TEN TOP SALES
TECHNIQUES
For Small Firms

To Ma and Pa, with fondest love

TEN TOP SALES TECHNIQUES
TECHNIQUES
For Small Firms

MAKE MORE MONEY BY
INCREASING SALES

NEIL JOHNSON

**KOGAN
PAGE**

Acknowledgements

Thanks to Aidan Hughes, my computer guru, for his no-nonsense technical advice; thanks also to Louise Barber for her invaluable commercial guidance.

The right of Neil Johnson to be identified as author of this work has been asserted by him in accordance with the Copyright, Designs and Patents Act 1988.

First published in 1995

Kogan Page Limited
120 Pentonville Road
London N1 9JN

© Neil Johnson 1995

British Library Cataloguing in Publication Data
A CIP record for this book is available from the British Library.

ISBN 0 7494 1837 0

Typeset by JS Typesetting, Wellingborough, Northants.
Printed in England by Clays Ltd, St Ives plc.

Contents

Introduction

- *Every working day, nearly 1000 small firms cease trading because they do not sell enough to pay their bills.*
- *If you want your small business to make money: learn how to sell!*

This book teaches you everything you need to know about selling.

This book contains ten simple sales techniques and over 100 practical examples that explain everything you need to know, in order to boost the sales of your small business.

This book is written by a small-business owner.

I know how it feels:
— to run a small business that no one has heard of;
— to be owed money by everyone;
— to have to be in four different places at once!

If this sounds like you and your business, then this is the book for you!

The ideas in this book will help you to boost your sales.

No matter what sort of small business you have, the ideas in this book will help you to sell more. For example, they helped me to boost the monthly sales of a small business from £5,000 to over £100,000.

Who will benefit from reading this book?

- Anyone who runs any sort of small firm (ie, with fewer than ten employees);
- Any sole trader;
- Any self-employed professional;
- Anyone with a commercial hobby or part-time business;
- Anyone who is thinking of setting up in business;
- Anyone who wants to learn how to sell.

The terms used in this book

Gender

In order to make this book as readable as possible, I have chosen to avoid writing 'he/she', 'him/her', 'his/her' whenever gender is mentioned. Instead, I usually attribute a single gender to my 'customers' to allow the text to flow without interruption. This is done purely for stylistic reasons. Thus the words 'he', 'him' and 'his' are at all times interchangeable with the words 'she', 'her' and 'hers', and vice versa.

'Product' means 'product or service'

The word 'product' is nearly always interchangeable with the words 'product' or 'service', and the word 'customer' with the word 'buyer'.

1

Find out what your customer wants

This is the most important sales technique you will ever learn.

No matter what you are selling or who you are selling it to, your first objective is always the same: *find out what your customer wants, ie, needs or requires.*

- Why is it so important to find out what your customer wants?
  Because unless you know what your customer wants, you cannot tell him how you can help.
- How do you find out what your customer wants?
  Ask, ask and ask again!
- What is the quickest way to lose a sale?
  The quickest way to lose a sale is to start selling something to a customer before you know what he wants.

If you don't ask customers what they want, you will lose sales

Charlie is a self-employed carpenter. One evening he visits a customer's house to quote for the job of making a new front door. The customer has everything organised. He explains the type of door he wants and gives Charlie a handwritten sketch. Charlie then takes the necessary measurements, thanks the customer and leaves. Later he calculates his quotation (it comes to £400) and pops it in the post to the customer. He never hears another word. Why not?

What is Charlie's mistake?
Because he does not ask, he thinks that the customer's *only* concern is to have a particular type of door installed. In fact, the customer's main concern is price; he wants to spend a maximum of £300.

What should Charlie have done?
Before leaving, Charlie should have asked one or two important questions to clarify the customer's concerns. For example, he should have asked:

- How much do you want to spend? or
- What's the most you want to spend?

By doing this, Charlie would have immediately discovered that the customer's maximum budget was £300. He could then have done one of two things: either he could have set a price below £300, or, if the type of door required was much more expensive than the customer's budget of £300, he could have suggested some cheaper alternatives.

The moral? First ask, then quote!

Andrew owns a small hardware store. A customer comes into his shop and chooses a brand of wood varnish. As it happens, the brand he chooses is old stock and is less effective than a newer brand that has recently come on to the market. Although Andrew has several tins of this newer brand in stock, he decides to keep quiet because he wants to get rid of the old stock. The customer pays for the varnish, walks out of the shop and never returns. Why not?

What is Andrew's mistake?
Because he does not ask, he assumes that the customer *only* wants to buy a tin of varnish. He also thinks that the customer is not particular about what varnish he buys.
   In fact, the customer wants to buy several other items, but because he cannot find them and is too shy to ask, he says

nothing. Instead, he buys them from another shop further along the high street, where he also discovers that the varnish he has just bought is an older brand. Feeling unhappy at the service offered by Andrew, the customer decides not to buy from him again.

What should Andrew have done?
Before taking the customer's money, Andrew should first have asked the customer whether he needed anything else. By doing this, he would have made more sales, immediately!

Next, Andrew should have asked the customer what he was planning to use the varnish for. For example, if it was an important task, he could have recommended the newer varnish. If it was an ordinary task, he could have explained that although a newer varnish was available, the older varnish would do just as well. By adopting this approach, Andrew would have gained the customer's confidence and goodwill and so improved his chances of future sales.

The moral: First ask, then sell!

Camilla owns a small young firm that makes novelty mugs. One day, she telephones the buyer of a large department store (to whom she has recently sent written details plus a sample mug) to try and get an order. After introducing herself, she explains her product range briefly and describes the different designs.

'But will they sell?' asks the buyer. 'Definitely' replies Camilla, and to prove it, she repeats all her selling points: the mugs are well made, they have interesting designs, they are well packaged and they are perfectly priced. Finally, to clinch the sale, she offers the buyer an extra 10 per cent discount if he places an immediate order. The buyer declines her offer. Why?

What is Camilla's mistake?
She thinks that the buyer's question (Will your mugs sell?) shows that he is *only* concerned about the *sellability* of her mugs. In fact, the buyer's question is really a smokescreen. His *real* concern is the reliability of Camilla's young company; ie, is it

capable of supplying the level of service required? So, while Camilla tries desperately to show how fast her mugs will sell, the buyer's real concern goes unanswered.

What should Camilla have done?
Before rushing to answer the buyer's question, she should have checked whether this was his real concern (eg, by asking something like: 'Is this your only concern?', or 'Is there anything else that worries you?'). By reacting in this manner, Camilla would have had a better chance of pinpointing what the buyer *really* thought.

The moral? First ask, then answer!

Never assume you know what a customer wants: always ask!

This is the basic difference between amateurs and professionals. Amateur salespeople think they know what customers want. Professional salespeople *ask* customers what they want.

The difference between amateurs and professionals

A customer telephones two different building firms to quote for the job of repairing his garage roof. The first is owned by *Arnie*, an amateur salesperson. The second is run by *Pat*, a professional. Compare the different sales approach of both men.

The telephone call

Amateur approach. When the customer phones, Arnie is out. His wife takes down the customer's address and says that Arnie will be there sometime after 2 pm the following day (Saturday).

Professional approach. Pat is also out when the customer phones, however, *his* wife not only asks for the customer's address, she also asks a few questions about the job, for instance, what type of roof is it? How big is the repair? When does he want the job done? Finally, she says that Pat will be there at 4 pm the next day.

The visit to the customer's house

Amateur approach. At 2.30 pm, Arnie the Amateur arrives at the house, inspects the garage roof, takes various measurements and jots down the details in his notebook. He then goes inside to have a quick word with Mr Customer. He explains that he has finished looking at the roof and that 'it looks a fairly straightforward job'. 'How much is it likely to cost?' asks Mr Customer. 'Oh I couldn't tell you that right now' says Arnie, 'I'll have to look at the figures. Can I give you a ring in a couple of days?' The customer agrees and Arnie leaves.

Professional approach. Pat arrives at 4 pm. He also inspects the garage roof and takes measurements. However, unlike Arnie, Pat is not simply content to find out what *needs* doing, he wants to find out *what the customer himself wants doing*. He therefore asks the customer himself to show him the garage roof and explain exactly what he wants doing.

Then, while they are both outside looking at the roof, Pat asks the customer more about the job. Does he simply want the roof to look good, or does he want a thorough repair? (Answer: a thorough repair.) Pat then sees that the roof at the rear of the garage (which needs no repair) has no guttering. As a result, the wall underneath is turning green from damp. He shows this to the customer and recommends putting in new guttering before the problem gets any worse. The customer, who has not noticed this before, agrees wholeheartedly.

Next, as they return to the front of the garage, Pat notices that the garage door is on its last legs. He asks the customer whether he wants him to quote for a replacement. 'That's not a bad idea' says the customer, 'my wife is always having trouble with it.'

Finally, Pat asks the customer two questions: first, ideally how much does he want to spend? (Answer: no more than £1000.) Second, how soon would he like a quote? (Answer: as soon as possible.) Luckily, thanks to his wife's earlier questioning of the customer, Pat has been able to prepare some of the costs before even arriving at the customer's house. He therefore gives the customer an approximate quote on the spot. He quotes £1100 for the roof and £300 for the door.

The quote is higher than the customer expects but, because he feels comfortable with Pat's approach, he accepts. Two days later, Arnie telephones with his own quote, only to be told that the job has gone elsewhere.

The moral? Because Pat is a professional salesperson, he talks to his customers to pinpoint exactly what they want. By contrast, because Arnie is an amateur, he never really bothers to ask customers what they want and so he never finds out!

What a customer wants will determine what he buys

Customers buy things in order to satisfy their individual needs or desires. Usually they have one thing in mind (eg, safety); sometimes they have more than one (eg, appearance and cost).

Your first task is to find out what your customer's particular concern is. If you can do this, you are well on the way towards making a sale.

What buyers usually want

1. **Retail buyers.** Ideally, these buyers want to buy products that:
    - will sell;
    - can be sold at a high profit;
    - are well advertised;
    - are well packaged;
    - carry point-of-sale inducements (eg, stickers or labels, well-flagged competitions etc);
    - don't age;
    - store easily;

- are supported by good service (eg, delivery);
- carry minimal risk (eg, that can be returned to the supplier if they don't sell).

2. **Other buyers.** Whether they are buying for themselves or for their company, you may expect most buyers to be concerned about one or more of the following:
   - **Risk/Overall Service.** Can you and your firm provide an adequate standard of service – including after-sales service?
   - **Reliability.** How often will your product break down?
   - **Performance.** Will your product do the job?
   - **Value For Money.** Is your product available elsewhere, cheaper? What are its operating costs, etc?
   - **Payment Terms.** What credit do you offer?

3. **House-owners (buying services from tradespeople).** House-owners are usually concerned with the following:
   - **Performance.** Can you do the job?
   - **Reliability.** Can you be trusted to do a good job?
   - **Value For Money.** Are your prices reasonable?
   - **Convenience.** Can you start straightaway? Will you finish the job reasonably quickly? Will you leave a mess?

How to find out what your customer wants

Prepare a list of questions to ask customers

Be prepared! Have some questions ready to help pinpoint the customer's requirements. Obviously, what you ask will depend on what (and to whom) you are selling. Here are some suggestions for two common situations – selling to other firms, and selling to private individuals.

If you sell xyz products to other firms

When you sell to other firms, try to ask as many questions as possible. For example, try asking:

1. What exactly does your company do?
2. Who do you sell to?/Who buys from you?
3. Have you bought any xyz before?
4. How much xyz do you usually use? Who do you buy it from?
5. What sort of results does it give you?
6. May I ask roughly how much you pay for it?
7. How important is xyz to your company?
8. How does it help your image, efficiency? operation?
9. When it comes to buying xyz . . . what importance do you place on: performance? reliability? convenience? speed of delivery? discount? sale or return? after-sales service?
10. Of these, which is the most important?
11. What sort of discount do you usually look for?
12. What special quality do you look for in your suppliers?

If you sell trade services to private customers

When visiting a house to quote for a trade job (eg, a building/plumbing/carpentry/general repair or maintenance job), always ask questions like:

1. What exactly do you want doing?
2. How long do you want it to last? (ie, what sort of quality is the customer looking for? – adequate or high quality?)
3. When do you want it done?
4. Can you give me an idea of how much you want to spend?/What is your maximum budget?
5. Have you had this sort of thing done before?

> NB: • *Study these questions carefully. Adapt them to your own particular situation and type of business.*
> • *Notice the use of open questions beginning with key words like, how, what, who, where, when, to stop your*

customer from denying you information by answering simply Yes or No.

Lottie owns a small firm that makes bangles and bracelets. She telephones the jewellery buyer for a chain of stores.

After introducing herself and her firm, Lottie explains that she would like to make an appointment to see the buyer. The buyer is not impressed and tries to give Lottie the push-off. Instead of responding by telling the buyer how wonderful her bangles are, Lottie asks one simple question:

'I get the feeling that you think I might be wasting your time, Mr Buyer, so before I go any further, may I ask what you think the biggest problem is likely to be, about buying my bangles?'

The buyer then explains quite bluntly that he only deals with large suppliers. He says he hates dealing with small firms, because they tend to be disorganised and unreliable.

Lottie is not sure what the buyer means, so she asks another question: 'Do you mean that you *would* deal with me but only if you were satisfied that my firm was reliable and properly organised?'

The buyer says that he might deal with her under those conditions, but he doubts whether she will ever be able to convince him. Lottie then says:

'I understand exactly what you're saying, but my firm *is* organised and I have the evidence to prove it. All I need is 20 minutes of your time to show you what I mean. How does that sound?'

The buyer is still reluctant to give way, but – since Lottie does not sound like a time-waster – he decides to give her a chance. He therefore fixes an appointment to see her. However, having succeeded in getting an appointment, *Lottie does not simply hang up!* Instead she takes the opportunity to ask a few more questions, to find out more about her customer. She says: 'While I'm on the phone can I just ask . . .

- How many stores do you have?
- How do your jewellery departments vary in size?
- What sort of jewellery do you sell most of?

- What price range is the most popular with your customers?
- What do you require from your suppliers in the way of display material? (eg do you prefer to use your *own* display stands?)
- What sort of discount do you usually look for?'

Since the main decision (to give Lottie an appointment) has already been taken, the buyer is now more relaxed and actually enjoys telling Lottie about how his stores operate and how he buys.

> *The moral? By concentrating solely on the priorities of her customer and by asking him as many questions as she dares, Lottie now knows exactly what he wants. Therefore, when she meets him, she will be able to tell him exactly how she can help.*

Finally, note how she never mentions her bangles and bracelets. Finding out her buyer's priorities is her only concern.

Conclusion: selling is easy once you know what your customers want

Many salespeople are their own worst enemy. Why? Because they never bother to find out what their customers want. Don't make the same mistake! *Listen* to your customer and try to find out what he's looking for and why.

Once you have done this, you will then know *what* to sell him and (more importantly) *how* to sell it to him.

This is the No 1 sales technique: the foundation of all selling. Study it carefully: it will make you a lot of money.

2

Explain how you can help

Once you have pinpointed your customer's particular requirement, your next task is to explain to him how you can help; ie, how your product or service will give him what he wants.

Match your explanation to the customer

To do this, draw your customer's attention to those features of your product which you *know* will satisfy his particular concern.

• If *Anthony's* priority is reliability, tell him how reliable it is; don't tell him how cheap it is.
• If *Beatrix* is concerned about the performance of your product, reassure her about performance; don't start talking about your after-sales service.
• If *Chris* is mainly interested in reselling your product as quickly as possible, show him what a fast-seller it is; don't bother explaining how well made it is.
• If *Davinia* is more interested in the snob-value of buying your product, tell her how your product will enhance her status and impress her friends; don't tell her what good value it is.
• If *Ebenezer* has more than one concern, deal with the more important one first.

Tip: If a customer raises an objection during your sales presentation, do not answer it! Instead, say you will deal with it at the end.

21

Your presentation should change according to the customer

As the above examples show, *how* you explain your product should always vary according to *who* your customer is. Never fall into the lazy habit of explaining your product to all your customers in the same way. Why not? Because each customer is only interested in how your product satisfies *his particular concern.*

How to explain your product or service

Since every customer is slightly different and will have a slightly different concern, be prepared to explain your product in many different ways. To help you, here are some simple suggestions on how to handle four typical concerns.

When your customer's main concern is the <u>small size of your firm</u>

Try to explain:

1. *How you have impressed other customers.*
   Prove it, by quoting details of (a) orders; (b) repeat orders; (c) letters of satisfaction received from these customers.

2. *How your small size gives the customer more individual attention.*
   Prove it, by giving details of how you/your partner will personally supervise the customer's account to ensure nothing goes wrong. Compare this with how larger companies operate.

3. *Why your small size means better service for the customer.*
   Prove it, by showing how you can respond faster than larger suppliers; eg, because you have fewer customers to look after, because you are local, or because, by specialising in

this particular field, you can offer the customer more expertise.

4. *How your product itself more than compensates for your size.*
   Prove it, with hard evidence; eg, samples, details of how your firm operates, evidence of work done (before/after photos etc).

5. *How you can help your customer to minimise the risk.*
   If the customer is worth it, offer him sale or return or a free trial or extra discount – but only as a last resort!

Aidan runs his own small computer consultancy. He installs computers and software systems in small- and medium-sized firms. One day, he visits Jack who is the MD of a large fruit importer.

Jack explains that he is thinking of installing a new computer but if he did, his main priority would be service and support. Because his company works all through the night, he needs to know that the computer firm he chooses is capable of handling any problems that might arise – 24 hours a day. Frankly, he doubts whether Aidan's firm has the resources to cope.

To satisfy this concern, Aidan adopts the following approach:

1. He produces three letters from other customers for whom he has installed computers. Each letter speaks glowingly of his service and efficiency. Conclusion: no need to worry about service.

2. He explains that most service engineers employed by large companies tend to be far less qualified than himself. Thus, since he does all the maintenance work himself, he can actually offer a better service than most larger companies. This means that Jack has even less to worry about.

3. He explains that being small is an advantage. For example, by having fewer customers to look after, his firm actually has *greater* flexibility (than a larger company) to respond to problems around the clock. He quotes a specific example of how he tackled a 3 am emergency repair that helped one customer to save thousands of pounds. All you have to do

is call me on this, (he says, pulling out his mobile phone) and you can rest assured that your problem will be solved, fast!

4. He also points out that he is reasonably local, which means that he will probably be able to respond faster than any national firm. He says that he usually responds to a call within two to three hours.

5. He explains that prevention is always better than cure. Most computer breakdowns occur as a result of faulty handling by their operators. This is why, after installing a computer system, he always spends extra time teaching its operators exactly how to operate it. This leads to more competent staff and fewer breakdowns, he says.

When your customer's main concern is <u>sellability</u>

This is the situation when you are selling to a retail customer.
  Try to explain:

1. *How the design of your product helps it sell.*
    Prove it (a) with details of your product's popular design/ impressive performance/competitive price/attractive packaging; (b) by demonstrating a sample of your product.

2. *How successful your product has been in other markets.*
    Prove it, by quoting the relevant details.

3. *How successful your product has been in UK tests/trials.*
    Prove it, by quoting the relevant details and/or letters of reference. Give details of any market research surveys etc.

4. *How you have impressed other customers of similar size.*
    Prove it, by showing letters of satisfaction.

5. *Which other customers buy your product.*
    Prove it, by giving a specific example.

6. *How you intend to support your product.*
    Prove it, by giving details of any advertising, point of sale material, special display stands etc.

7. *How you can help your customer to minimise the risk.*
   If the customer is worth it, offer him sale or return or a free trial or extra discount – but only as a last resort!

Lottie owns a small firm that makes bangles and bracelets. She visits the jewellery buyer for a chain of stores and, after convincing him not to be put off by the small size of her firm, she discovers that he has *another* major concern; ie, whether her bangles will sell. This is Lottie's reply:

1. She says that her bangles are very carefully designed, ie,
   — they are very competitively priced (£1.99–£6.99);
   — they are highly visible (ie, very brightly coloured);
   — they are based upon a brand new and very popular US design;
   — they have a desirable 'French' brand name ('Bardot');
   Conclusion: her bangles are likely to be snapped up!

2. She shows the buyer a recent article from a UK women's magazine, which states that a major US firm is planning to start selling similar bangles in the UK, priced at £12.99. She says that this proves that there is a serious demand for this type of product and that hers will seem exceptional value by comparison. Conclusion: her bangles will sell like hot cakes!

3. Although she has not sold any bangles to any other chain-stores, this fact actually benefits the customer! How? Because *his* chain-store won't have to compete with any other store, at least for the moment. Conclusion: her bangles will sell faster!

4. She produces evidence of orders (and reorders) from other smaller customers. Conclusion: her bangles sell!

5. She produces samples of her bangles together with a small display unit (which comes free of charge). She explains that the buyer is the first customer for whom the stand has been made available, thus her previous sales were achieved with no proper display. Conclusion: her sales are almost certain to improve!

NB: At this stage, Lottie makes no offer of sale or return, or any sort of free trial. Although she is desperate to sell to the buyer, she prefers to wait and see how he reacts, before committing herself.

When your customer's main concern is <u>reliability</u>

Try to explain:

1. *How rarely your product breaks down.*
   Prove it, with written evidence. Refer to your brochure etc.

2. *How you have impressed other customers of similar size.*
   Prove it, by showing letters of satisfaction.

3. *How efficient your after-sales service is.*
   Prove it, by explaining exactly how your service works.

4. *How quick your firm is to replace defective items.*
   Prove it, by quoting specific examples.

5. *How you guarantee your product.*
   Prove it, by producing a copy of your guarantee.

6. *How you can help the customer to minimise the risk.*
   If the customer is worth it, offer him sale or return or a free trial or extra discount – but only as a last resort!

Fast Eddie owns a small removals firm, with two transit vans. He meets Ziggy (a concert-promoter) to convince him to use the Fast Eddie Removal Service to transport equipment around the Midlands and the north of England, for his next series of concerts. After Ziggy indicates that his main requirement is reliability, Fast Eddie responds as follows:

First, he produces references from two wrestlers – Bone Crusher Bill and The Mad Axeman – whose stage props he recently ferried around England without mishap. He also produces a copy of a recent letter from Worldwide Events Ltd, thanking him for work done in connection with the British Golf Championship. These letters prove his reliability, he says.

Second, he explains some of his background. After six years in the army, he left to start his own messenger service armed with just one old bicycle. He then bought a motorbike, then two, then a van. Now he has two vans and enough work to consider buying a third. What's more, he never advertises: all his business comes from personal recommendation. That's reliability, he says.

Third, he explains how he operates. He uses three other drivers – two of whom have been with him for the past eight years – and all are teetotal as well as being qualified mechanics. Conclusion: his removal service is both reliable *and* self-sufficient.

Fourth, he produces the service logs of both vans. They show two years of regular maintenance. The last time he had a breakdown or missed an appointment, was during a blizzard five years ago, when even British Rail failed to keep going. That sort of reliability is hard to beat, says Fast Eddie.

Fifth, he says that no one can guarantee 100 per cent reliability. The best you can do is to show how your service operates when things go wrong. He then shows Ziggy a filofax containing a list of 60 garages, from John o'Groats to Lands End. He explains that he knows many of the owners personally. These names are his ultimate guarantee of reliability.

When your customer's main concern is <u>performance</u>

Try to explain:

1. *How your product is perfect for the job.*
    Prove it, by quoting those specific features that demonstrate how your product can help the customer *in his situation.*

2. *How your expertise/resources are right for the job.*
    Prove it, by quoting your own and your firm's experience in your particular field. Add any further details of technical qualifications etc, and other technical back-up facilities.

3. *How your product has helped other customers of similar size.*
    Prove it, by giving details plus evidence (eg, before/after photos, letters of satisfaction etc).

4. *How you guarantee the performance of your product.*
    Prove it, by giving details of (a) your product's overall reliability, (b) your product guarantee, (c) your after-sales service, (d) your firm's willingness and proven ability to cope with all the most likely problems.

Slim is a slow-moving 45 year old who runs a small painting and decorating business with a partner and two juniors. One day he visits Mr Dynamite, the manager of a local nursing home that looks as if it could do with redecorating. Mr Dynamite agrees that the place needs smartening up, but questions whether Slim has the ability to do it fast enough to minimise inconvenience to guests. This is how Slim presents his case.

First, he slowly produces a packet of letters from his inside pocket. The packet contains 30 letters from a variety of satisfied customers, including two other local nursing homes – Slim says that he prefers to let his customers testify to his painting skills.

Second, he points out that both the other nursing homes needed a quick job done for the same reason. They were perfectly satisfied, he says. Conclusion: he can do the job!

Third, he emphasises that the best way of reducing the inconvenience of having ladders and paint-pots around the place is to employ painters who know their job; ie, who will do the sort of professional job that won't need repainting in 18 months. Since between them he and his partner have more than 40 years' experience of painting, they know exactly how to do a fast, efficient and tidy job.

Finally, he explains that (unlike most firms he knows), he guarantees his work; ie, if any of his paintwork is found to be faulty at any time over the next three years, he will repair the mistake free of charge. That is how confident he is of providing Mr Dynamite with the service he needs.

Checklist

- *Prepare like a professional*
  Remember, only amateurs rely on natural sales ability!
  Professionals rely on being prepared.

- *Customers only have a limited amount of time: don't waste it!*
  Don't make the mistake of waffling on about all the
  wonderful features of your product. Instead, focus
  specifically on the features that give the customer what he's
  looking for.

- *Explain your product by using the 1:2:3 Method*
  1. Make your point.
  2. Back it up with evidence.
  3. Show how this helps the customer.

- *Tip:* don't make your product sound perfect: you will only
  invite unnecessary objections.

- *Written evidence convinces customers – get some today!*
  One piece of written evidence is more effective than a
  thousand opinions. So start collecting some! Get hold of
  testimonials, references, 'before and after' photos of work
  done, market surveys, or even newspaper or magazine
  articles. You won't regret it!

3

Close the sale and get the order

Now comes, the nitty-gritty! Having explained your product to the customer, you must now *help him to make up his mind to buy it*. This final process is called closing the sale.

Successful closing is the result of your earlier efforts. Closing is the natural end to the sales sequence. If you have conducted the earlier parts of the sale well, you will usually find it relatively easy to close the sale. On the other hand, if you have mishandled your questioning or your presentation, you will encounter more resistance.

Help the buyer to make up his mind. Nearly 6 out of 10 of all sales presentations go unclosed. Why? Because (amazingly) many salespeople never get round to asking for the order. After explaining their product, they sort of expect the customer to suddenly say:

'That's fine then, here's a nice fat order for you.'

The truth is, most buyers need *help* with their buying decision. Your final task, therefore, is to help the buyer to take this decision. This is what closing a sale is all about.

Help your buyer to say Yes by being positive and confident. Nothing reassures a customer more than a salesperson who is positive about his product and confident that he (the customer) will buy it. Conversely, nothing worries a customer more than a salesperson who sounds doubtful or uncertain.

The moral: If you sound as though you assume the customer is going to buy, he might. If you sound doubtful, he won't.

Help your buyer to say Yes by giving him something to say Yes to!

Always offer the buyer something specific to buy, or several specific alternatives. For example:

- If you sell bangles, don't just offer the customer bangles; offer him a range of specific quantities – eg, 100 mixed, 200 mixed or 500 mixed.
- If you are selling your skills as an electrician, offer the customer a quotation (or contract) to sign.
- If you are selling your services as a children's music tutor, give the parent a form to sign, stipulating a set number of lessons.

How *not* to close the sale

Before I show you how to close a sale, let me show you how *not* to do it.

For instance, after explaining how your product meets your customer's requirements, *do not* say something like:

- Are you interested?
- What do you think?
- How do you feel about all that?
  (These three questions are too general – who cares how the customer feels? *What you need to know is – will he buy?*)
- Do you think it's worth buying?
- Would you like to place an order?
  (This type of question puts too much pressure on the average buyer to take the decision for himself. It invites the standard reply: 'Er. . . I'll have to think about it.')
- Do you want to decide now or would you rather have a think about it?
  (Never give your buyer the opportunity to postpone a decision. What you are really saying is: it's OK by me if you'd rather not say Yes. *It's not OK!*)

How to close the sale successfully

Here are four effective ways to close the sale. Study them carefully, and adapt them to your particular business.

The take-it-for-granted close

As the name suggests, this is where you simply take it for granted that your customer is going to give you an order.

So, after you have finished explaining how your product meets his requirements, instead of asking him *whether* he wants to buy it, you ask *how much* he wants or *when* he wants it.

Say something like:

- So, when would you like me to start? How about next Monday?
- So, if you just sign here, I can put things in motion.
- So, how about giving me a trial order? Would 200 be enough?
- So, can I put you down for (say) 200?
- So look, let's go ahead shall we, and I'll get a delivery out to you . . . say Thursday? Will Thursday suit you?
- So, assuming we go ahead with this, where would you like it delivered?
- So, assuming everything is agreed, who should I send the paperwork to? Who handles the details at your end?

In effect, you take the buyer's decision for him. Amazingly, this is often a great relief to many buyers.

The alternative close

This is a variant of the take-it-for-granted close. Once again, instead of asking your customer whether he wants to buy your product, you ask *which of your products* he wants – the x version or the y version.

Say something like:

- Well, now that you've heard about our three basic products and how they can solve your problem, Mr Buyer, which do you prefer? The standard, the medium or the de luxe?
- From what I've just said, which of your products do you think will suit you best? The red one or the black one?
- Bearing everything in mind, which product would you like to try, the round one or the square one?

As in the previous close, you are switching the buyer's attention from the big decision (ie, *whether* to buy) to a relatively minor decision (ie, *which one* to buy).

The special-offer close

In this closing method, use the incentive of a special offer to help the buyer say Yes, today! You can also combine it with the alternative close.

Say something like:

- Since this is going to be your first order with us, Mr Brown, you get a special *half-price* introductory offer – everything is half-price on this one order. Shall I put you down for 100 or 200?
- If you buy now Mr Smith, you get 25 per cent off everything, so why don't I put you down for 100?
- I'll tell you what Mr Bloggs, give me an order for the blue one now and I won't charge you for delivery. How's that?

NB: *As always, you must assume the buyer is going to buy.*

The what-have-you-got-to-lose close

Use this on customers who stubbornly refuse to buy, for no good reason.

Start by telling your customer that:

- You understand his priority (eg, reliability).
- You have demonstrated how reliable your product is.
- You have shown him testimonials from other customers that prove how reliable it is, in practice.
- You have explained how you guarantee your product and how you provide an effective after-sales service.

In other words, you have demonstrated that his risk is minimal, yet he is still not satisfied.

Then say to him:

- Tell me, Mr Buyer, *what have you got to lose* by giving me an order?

In my experience, most customers faced with this question either explain what bothers them – in which case you should resell them your product accordingly – or they still refuse to buy but start showing you a bit more respect. I remember one customer in particular, who listened to me in complete silence over the phone, and then said: 'well, if you feel that strongly, you'd better come and see me.' The following week, I duly went to see him and came away with a large order!

Some customers decide to buy immediately, others take longer

Some buyers take decisions easily and quickly, others don't.

So what? If you can't close the sale today, close it tomorrow or next week, or next month – just because a buyer needs more time, don't assume that all is lost. Keep perservering: experts say that 75 per cent of people will buy if they are asked five times!

How to handle customer objections

However you conduct the sale, many customers will still object to *something*. Fortunately, most objections are easily predictable. In my experience, three-quarters of all objections boil down to one of these five different statements:

- I don't think your company can offer me the service I need.
- I don't think your product is fully reliable.
- I don't think your product can solve my problem.
- I don't think your product will sell.
- I don't think your product is good value.

> *The moral? Prepare answers to these five different points and you will be able to answer 75 per cent of all objections!*

The professional method of handling objections

The most effective way to handle objections is to use the method which is recommended in most professional training manuals. It consists of four stages;

1. Welcome the objection
2. Clarify it
3. Test it
4. Answer it.

Welcome the objection

When a customer objects, most amateur salespeople get defensive and immediately try to justify themselves. By contrast, professionals immediately *welcome* the objection – no matter how stupid it may be. They say things like:

— I'm glad you raised that . . .
— That's a good point, I'm glad you mentioned it . . .
— I agree, that's important, thanks for bringing it up . . .

Why welcome the objection? Because it makes the customer feel good.

Clarify the objection

The professional next tries to discover what the customer means by his objection. For example, when a customer says something like: 'I'm sorry, you're just too expensive' he could mean any one of several different things:

- He can't afford to buy your product; or
- He needs credit; or
- Your product is not good value for money; or
- His budget is already used up; or
- He thinks that your product is not really suitable for him; or
- He is not really interested; or
- He is interested but wants to squeeze you for more discount.

Ask questions to clarify the objection. For example, ask things like:

- You say that you prefer to deal with larger firms; may I ask why, exactly?
- You say that you don't think my product is likely to sell. Can you be a little more precise?
- When you say that my product is too expensive, are you worried that it won't give you the results you want, or are you saying that you can buy cheaper elsewhere?
- When you say that your budget is already used up, do you mean that there's no more money, or do you mean that you're not yet convinced that my product is worth finding more money for?
- When you say that my quote is too expensive, what do you mean exactly?
- When you say that you need more time, is it because you're still not sure about the product, (find out why) or do you need to talk it over with someone? (find out who).

Why clarify the objection? Because until you know exactly what it's about, you cannot answer it properly.

Test the objection

Never answer an objection before you have tested it to see if it is genuine. Why not? Because it may simply be a cover for the real one. If it is, you will only waste time by answering it!

Use an 'if' question to test the objection. Here are some standard 'if' questions for you to adapt:

- *If* I can show you that my small firm is equally, if not more, reliable than most larger ones, will you give us a try?
- *If* I can prove to you that my product can solve your particular problem, will that convince you to buy?
- *If* I can show you that my product is likely to sell as well, if not better, than the main brands, will you give me an order?
- *If* I can show you that my product is more cost-effective than the one you're currently using, will that persuade you to switch?

Result? If the objection is genuine, the customer usually replies Yes, in which case you must now try to answer it well enough to reassure his concern once and for all.

If the objection is fake, the customer usually says No. However, as a rule, he also tells you his *real* objection, in which case you should welcome, clarify and test it all over again.

Answer the objection

Some objections can be answered by simply re-explaining the strength and suitability of your product. Others may require you to go into greater detail to convince the customer once and for all.

Aidan is trying to sell his computer installation service to Jack, who is worried about buying from a small firm. After presenting his case (see p 23), Aidan tries to close the sale but Jack objects: he's still not sure that a small firm can provide an adequate service. After welcoming, clarifying and testing the objection, Aidan finally answers it as follows:

- He produces a typed case history of one of his previous computer installations, which explains how he maintained the computer after it had been installed and, in particular, how he dealt with the problems that arose. It shows (a) why each problem occurred; (b) how quickly Aidan fixed it; and (c) how pleased the customer was with the result.
- Aidan takes Jack through the case history page by page, answering questions as he goes along. Finally, he suggests that Jack gives him a try. Jack agrees: his fears have disappeared.

Lottie is trying to sell her bangles to a chain-store buyer, who is worried about whether they will sell. After presenting her case (see p 25), she tries to close the sale but the buyer objects: he still doubts that Lottie's bangles can compete with established brands. After welcoming the objection, she answers it as follows:

- She produces a typed summary of a recent in-store customer survey, which was conducted in the jewellery section of a large northern department store. According to the survey, when shown a sample, 3 out of every 10 customers expressed an interest in Lottie's bangles. Of these, *half* expressed a strong desire to buy.
- Next, Lottie redemonstrates the features of her display case. She reminds the buyer that he will be the first customer to use it and stresses that her other sales have been achieved without the benefit of a good display. 'How many established brands would sell without a good display?' she asks.
- Finally, she suggests that the buyer place a trial order, and says that she will take back up to 20 per cent of all bangles that remain unsold at the end of three months. Lottie's arguments do the trick. The buyer agrees to a small trial order.

Fast Eddie is trying to sell his transport service to Ziggy (see p 26). After presenting his case, Eddie tries to close the sale but Ziggy objects: he is still worried about Eddie's reliability. After welcoming his concern, Eddie answers it as follows:

- He produces typed work sheets for both vans, showing what each van has done over the past month and the exact maintenance work that has been done on them. Both vans have been extremely busy and both have also been well looked after.
- As further proof, he also produces a letter from his local MOT garage, praising the roadworthiness of the vans.
- Next, by way of comparison, he tells Ziggy the story of what happened when he (Eddie) hired two vans from a national rental firm. The vans were badly maintained, they broke down and, on top of it all, the firm refused to refund the hire charges. He backs this up by showing Ziggy solicitor's letters on the matter.
- Finally, he says that if either of his vans break down and cause Ziggy any problems, he will refund Ziggy a week's charge. Ziggy is convinced and agrees to buy.

Slim is trying to sell his painting and decorating services to Mr Dynamite, who is worried about whether Slim can do the job quickly enough. After presenting his case (see p 28), Slim tries to close the sale but Mr Dynamite objects: he says he's still not convinced. Slim answers as follows:

- He produces two sets of 'before and after' photographs. The first set shows how Jimbo – one of Slim's two assistants – painted the complete outside of a house, for charity, in less than a day. The second set shows how Slim himself completed the entire inside of a local health clinic, during the course of a Sunday. He explains that both jobs were successfully completed against the clock, and produces two letters (one from the charity and one from the boss of the health clinic) to prove it.

- Mr Dynamite is convinced. He asks Slim to give him a quote as soon as possible.

How to handle objections concerning cost

Most price objections are fake

When a customer objects to buying your product and says something like: 'You're too expensive' or, 'I can't afford it', he usually means one of the following:

- I don't think your product will give me what I'm looking for;
- I don't think your product/firm is reliable enough;
- I don't think your product will sell.

Most price objections are really objections about other things, like reliability/performance/sellability and so on. So deal with these issues first before you start talking about price.

Woody owns a very successful small firm that sells mid-price office furniture. One day he has an appointment to see Alan, the MD of another small company that writes computer games for kids.

Unfortunately, Alan is in a rush and asks to see Woody's brochure immediately. He then looks through it for a few minutes, then says: 'Sorry Woody, but I can't afford anything like this.'

Woody doesn't bat an eyelid and responds as follows:

- First, he realises that now is not the time to argue. Alan is in too much of a rush. He says that he quite understands Alan's reaction, but he would like to call back at a more convenient time as he has something that will definitely interest him. Alan agrees and sets a new time. However, before Woody leaves, he quickly asks Alan a few questions about his business, eg, who he sells to, how many customers/suppliers visit his office etc.

- Next, armed with the answers to these questions, Woody prepares for his second appointment. He know that Alan's objection is not really about price: it is simply his way of saying: 'I don't see how buying this furniture is going to benefit me.' Thus, in order to convince Alan to buy, he knows that he has to show him exactly how new furniture will help to improve his business.
- So, at his second meeting, Woody begins by saying that no one buys his furniture because of its attractive looks or its comfort. The only reason people buy it is to make money. This immediately gets Alan's attention!
- He then produces a recent US survey which states that: the more professional a firm looks, the better treatment it receives from its suppliers and customers; ie, the firm gains more respect from both its suppliers (who give better service) and its customers (who buy more).
- Does it work in practice? Yes, says Woody. To prove it, he produces several letters from other customers, testifying to the increase in business that his furniture has brought them as a result of their improved 'company image'.
- Finally, he gives Alan a short typed report on what furniture to buy to improve his office layout, increase his usable space and upgrade his image. The report ends by itemising the practical savings that Alan will achieve. For example, Alan never invites customers to his office because it is too shabby. Instead, he arranges meetings in hotel conference rooms. By improving his office – which can then be used for meetings – he can significantly reduce his overheads. He will also save a great deal of time spent travelling to and from meetings: time that can now be used more profitably.
- Finally, new furniture with better storage capability will create more work space. This means greater efficiency and better working conditions for his staff (who will be happier and more motivated).

Woody tells Alan that when all these savings are taken into account, the real cost of the furniture is negligible. Alan says he will visit Woody's showroom the very next day!

The moral? When someone objects about price, it usually means that you have failed to convince him that your product is good enough; ie, he needs more proof that your product will give him the results he's looking for.

How to handle genuine price objections

If a customer is serious about buying your product but still says 'You're too expensive', he usually means one of three things:

- He can buy the same product more cheaply from another firm;
- Your product's performance does not justify its price; or
- He wants to squeeze you for extra discount.

Find out which he means, then give an appropriate answer.

If he can buy the same product more cheaply from another firm

First, question your customer:

- How much cheaper is it?
- Is it really the same product? Is it as good, as reliable etc?
- Does it come with the same level of after-sales service etc?
- Is it really cheaper? How long will it stay cheaper?
- How much is he thinking of buying from you?

Second, try to improve your competitiveness:

- Offer more product for the same price;
- Offer faster delivery or even better after-sales service etc;
- Offer a price-freeze for (say) two years;
- Offer extra discount in return for a large order or cash settlement;
- *Only as a last resort reduce your prices.*

If the performance of your product does not justify its price

First, question your customer:

- How much is he thinking of buying from you?
- Does he mean that he cannot take advantage of all the features of your product?
- How much cheaper can he buy the same product from another firm?

Second, try to show how your product can give him more benefits:

- Show him the specific financial advantages which your product offers, including those that he may not have considered;
- Offer more product for the same price;
- Offer faster delivery or even better after-sales service etc;
- Offer a price-freeze for (say) two years;
- Offer extra discount in return for a large order/cash terms;
- *Only as a last resort reduce your prices!*

If your customer wants to squeeze you for extra discount

First, question your customer:

- How much is he thinking of buying from you?
- How much discount does he want?
- Can he pay cash, or can he pay quickly, eg within seven days?

Second, offer him better terms:

- Offer more product for the same price;
- Offer faster delivery or even better after-sales service etc;
- Offer a price-freeze for (say) two years;
- Offer extra discount in return for a large order/cash terms;
- *Only as a last resort offer extra discount for nothing!*

Checklist

* *Make it easy for your customer to give you an order*
  — Ask him for the order!
  — Sound as though you expect him to buy!
  — Have a well-practised closing method up your sleeve!
* *Overcome any objections with the 1:2:3:4 Method*
  1. Welcome   2. Clarify   3. Test   4. Answer

Tip: If your customer avoids raising an obvious objection for which you have a good answer, raise it and answer it yourself!

* *Pay careful attention to objections about price*
  Remember: most price objections are usually objections about other things.

Tip: Because price is usually a secondary concern for most serious customers, try to postpone any mention of it until you have covered everything else.

* *Make it easy for the buyer to 'sell' your product to his colleagues*
  Many buyers need to consult with colleagues before they will give you a firm order. During these consultations, his colleagues may raise objections which he himself did not bother to raise with you. When this happens, the buyer will usually be obliged to recontact you for further discussions. **Result?** At best, the sale will be postponed; at worst, it will be lost altogether.

The moral? If your buyer indicates that he needs to consult his colleagues before committing himself, give him the answers to all likely objections. By doing this, you are making it easy for him to 'sell' your product to others.

4

How to turbo-charge your sales message

Make your sales message look professional!

It's not who you *are* that counts – it's who people *think you are!* If your sales message looks professional, people will think you are professional.

The importance of the written word

According to experts, when something is written down, it becomes more believable – eg, the Bible. They also say that the average listener only remembers about 10 per cent of a spoken explanation, whereas they remember up to 40 per cent of a written explanation. So what? So if you want your customers to remember what you tell them, make sure you give them written details!

Remember: buyers sometimes need to consult with colleagues. If a buyer has to consult with others before giving you a firm order, you will make his job a lot easier by supplying him with written details.

- *Buy some business stationery.*
  You must have your own business stationery. Why? Because without it, you can never contact customers in writing without looking like an amateur. If you don't have any, go to a high street print shop and buy some.

What sort should you buy? The sort that is right for your customers. For example, if your firm sells a luxury product or service, buy a top quality paper and have your details printed in coloured ink; otherwise, buy a medium quality paper and use black ink. Never choose a low quality paper (however cheap) – it makes you look like a cowboy outfit!

- *Buy a word-processor or typewriter.*
  Writing business letters by hand is a complete waste of time. Ideally, invest in a word processor, plus printer (from any electrical chain-store), or buy yourself a reliable typewriter with an automatic correction facility.

- *Print your invoices and delivery notes.*
  Printed forms always make you look more professional than numbered pages from a notebook. If you can't afford your own printed invoices, buy a set of standard printed invoices and stamp your name on them with a printing stamp (available from any high street print shop).

- *Include a sales message on all your stationery.*
  Put a small sales message next to your company name on all your stationery, eg 'The firm that offers real after-sales service', or 'The plumber who won't let you down', or 'The company that offers 24-hour delivery at no extra cost', or 'The company you can contact 7 days a week' . . . etc.

- *Design a single page reply letter for everyday use.*
  If you regularly receive a particular type of enquiry, design a standard letter which contains the information required (as well as information about how reliable and efficient your firm is) and then *send it out whenever you receive a similar enquiry* – even if you have already given the customer verbal details. Customers are always impressed with firms who bother to send written replies.

Marjorie owns a small curtain-fabric shop. One day, a lady phones to ask about a particular fabric. After taking the lady's details Marjorie explains that although the fabric is excellent, she has none left – it will be two weeks before she has a new delivery. The lady thanks Marjorie and says she will look elsewhere. Nevertheless, the following day, Marjorie sends the customer a standard letter outlining the shop's overall service. At the end, she adds a PS with details and prices of the fabric in question.

As it happens, the customer delays buying her curtains and, because Marjorie was the only person who bothered to send her written details, she eventually buys from Marjorie's shop.

- *Design a special thank you letter for everyday use!*
  If you want to be really clever, design some all-purpose thank you letters. Send them to customers who have bought a reasonable amount from you, or even to those who have bought nothing!

Gerard runs his own small damp-proofing company. So does *Shane*. One day they both visit a customer's house to quote for the job of damp-proofing some rear walls. Unfortunately, the customer gives the job to a third company, owned by Harry, an acquaintance of his. Because Shane is young and inexperienced, he thinks no more about the job-that-might-have-been. But Gerard is older and wiser. He immediately sends the customer a standard thank you letter, which (a) thanks the customer for his interest; (b) reminds him to get in touch if he ever has a similar problem; and (c) explains how efficient and reliable Gerard's firm is.

As it happens, Harry fails to turn up on the appointed day. The customer therefore phones Gerard (not Shane) and offers him the job instead. Why? Because he thinks that any firm that can be bothered to send a thank you letter is obviously more professional than one that doesn't.

Five different ways to get your sales message across

In order to present your sales message to customers in the most professional way, you *must* have your own sales literature. Choose what you can afford from the following list, and don't be too mean! In my experience, sales literature pays for itself many times over.

1. *A professionally printed brochure.*
    A printed brochure may be expensive but it can make all the difference between winning an order and getting the brush-off. Use it as your No 1 sales aid and give a copy to every *serious* customer you come across. (*Tip: when you post some-one a brochure, always include a covering letter. Why? Everyone reads covering letters!*) Brochure costs vary, so shop around. Expect to pay £500+ for 500 copies of a four-page, full colour brochure, including design and artwork costs.

2. *A standardised sales letter/series of letters.*
    If you can't afford a printed brochure, use standardised sales letters instead. If you don't have your own word-processor, go to any secretarial service company and ask them to produce what you want, on theirs (prices vary). If you sell only one type of product, you will probably need just one basic letter; if you offer more, you will probably need more letters.

    The bad news is, standard sales letters will not make you look as professional as a printed brochure will; the good news is, they are much more flexible (you can design different letters for different products, or for different types of customer). They also cost a fraction of the price of a brochure so you can be less choosy about who to give them to. You can also amend them much more easily. (*Tip: always include a PS at the end of your letter: people* always *read PS's!*)

Mimi owns a shop that sells sewing machines; knitting machines; sewing accessories; knitting accessories; and offers a garment-repair service. To help sell these five products, she uses five different sales letters – one for each product. She uses these letters whenever she sends out a mailshot to previous customers, when replying to mail-order enquiries, or when customers visit the shop in person.

Valentino owns a small hotel. Recently, he has converted some of the bedrooms into business conference rooms and is about to start selling this service to local firms. To do this, he has prepared a very expensive brochure, which he intends to send out only to managing directors of large or medium-sized companies.

However, to generate maximum publicity within these companies, he also needs to send details to their sales and personnel directors; furthermore, he knows he can't afford to ignore smaller companies – they, too, must be contacted. To do this, he designs three different sales letters: one aimed at sales directors (which talks about how he can stage sales-conferences); one aimed at personnel directors (which explains how he can stage private interviews); and one aimed at small firms (which explains how any small company can use his overall facilities to look big). **Result?** He gets maximum publicity without wasting a single expensive brochure.

3. *Leaflets.*
   Besides being cheap, leaflets are very visually effective and they are multi-purpose – you can hand them to customers, pop them in letter-boxes, give them out in the street, or put them up on walls and shop windows.

   They are ideal for selling a particular item (a new product) or promoting a specific event (a sale) but, unlike brochures or sales letters, they are not usually retained for future use by their recipients. Take a rough design to any printer, and expect to pay about £150 for 1000 copies. *Tip: use bright coloured paper – the brighter the better – and keep text to a minimum.*

4. *Photographs of your firm, your product, your work.*
   One picture is worth a thousand words, remember? So save yourself a lot of talking and get a professional photographer to take some impressive snaps that you can show to customers! Cost: about £15 per hour, plus travelling expenses, plus developing costs.

   Photos make ideal sales aids for any craftsman (to

demonstrate work done) or for any firms with visually attractive products, or for just about anyone who wants to make an impression. And yet despite this, very few small firms seem to use them!

Ruby owns a small market-research company. As part of her sales presentation to customers, she always produces a photo of her firm's office. This shows a modern, immaculately tidy, computerised office, with four telephones manned by well-groomed young people who look thoroughly professional. This photo creates the clearest possible impression of a young, up-to-date and professional organisation. What's more, by allowing customers to 'see inside' her company, Ruby demonstrates the sort of openness that gives her a definite edge over her competitors.

5. *Videos – the ultimate sales aid.*
    If you can afford to go the whole hog, contact a video production company and have a video made of your firm. Expect to pay about £3000+ for a five-minute video – this will include one day's filming at one location; 100 copies will cost about £250.

    However, remember that not all customers will have TVs and video recorders on which to view your video. You may have to lug your own around with you!

How to write a sales brochure that sells

Many business people still think that the purpose of a sales brochure is to promote the name of their firm and to explain what it does. This is wrong. From start to finish, the purpose of your sales brochure is to *sell your product*; ie, instead of telling customers *what you do*, you should tell customers *why they should buy your product!* Here's how to do it:

Use a front cover headline

Start by grabbing the attention of the reader with an effective headline on the front cover. For example:

Hannibal owns Impact Ltd, a small firm that makes promotional videos for companies. His brochure is headlined: 'How An Impact Video Will Make Money For Your Company – Dial 01–234–566 for a free quote without obligation'.

Astrid owns Office Help Ltd, a small company that offers secretarial services to other small firms. Her brochure is headlined: '6 Reasons Why You Should Call Office Help, Today!'

Highlight your benefits

Highlight the benefits that your customers will receive, by buying your product. List them in order of importance and *number* them!

> *Tips:* • *Use bold headings;*
> • *Support them with detail, but not too much;*
> • *Use language that appeals to the reader (eg, words like 'You' and 'Your');*
> • *Where possible, use good clear photos/drawings (with captions!) to illustrate your points.*

Hannibal's brochure lists six benefits:

1. *Increased competitiveness!*
   By having a professional video made of your company, you immediately stand out from your rivals. **Result?** You gain a competitive edge.

2. *Increased sales!*
   A video makes you look much more professional and because you look professional, customers will think you *are*

professional and will buy more **Result?** Your sales will go up.

3. *Increased profits!*
    As customers start taking you more seriously, you will find it easier to maintain (and increase) your prices. **Result?** Your profits will go up.

4. *Lower costs!*
    You can also use your video to impress suppliers, in order to obtain more credit, higher discounts and longer repayment terms. **Result?** Your costs will go down.

5. *Guaranteed quality for money!*
    Our customers include several large companies and all our videos are made to the highest technical specification. **Result?** You are guaranteed the highest possible video quality.

6. *Guaranteed value for money!*
    Our video prices are the best available. We will match any lower price. **Result?** You are guaranteed value for money.

Outline your evidence

*   Outline the names/types of customers who currently buy from you.
*   Use any comments or testimonials from satisfied customers.
*   Quote any official reports, market surveys, newspaper articles.
*   Use illustrative charts, graphs or photos.

Hannibal's brochure quotes the following evidence:

*   A recent highly respected UK market survey, which concludes that companies who use promotional videos achieve higher sales and profits than those who don't.

- Extracts from six letters from satisfied customers, testifying to the increase in sales/profits that has resulted from using a video to promote their company and their products.

Show how you minimise the risk to your customer

- Give details of your guarantee.
- Give details of how you respond to complaints.
- Give details of your after-sales service.
- Quote other customers who are pleased with your service.

Hannibal's brochure lists a number of possible risks, then explains how his firm deals with them. For example (in brief):

Q: How do you know whether your firm needs a video?
A: We offer a free consultation and expert advice.
Q: How do you know what type of video suits you best?
A: Use our large video library, which shows all types.
Q: How can you be sure that your video will contain the things you want?
A: You have full control at all times over what is filmed.
Q: How do you know that your video will work for you?
A: Ask our other customers! (Hannibal encloses a list.)

Get your customer to act

- Tell your customer to contact you, today!
- Give your phone and/or fax number and be in to take the call!
- Always include a form (ideally a pre-paid card) which enables the customer to order your product or to ask you to call.
- Ideally, give the customer an incentive to respond.

Hannibal's brochure offers all customers who reply, a free video entitled: 'Professional Video-making in 6 Easy Stages'. This explains exactly how a video is made and how good Hannibal's firm is at making one.

Low cost sales brochures for the self-employed

No matter what type of skilled person you are, you can (and should) have some sort of sales brochure. Even if your regular customers know all about you, you will always meet new customers who don't. Here is a simple suggestion to help you to improve your sales message to these new customers.

1. Use a brightly coloured leaflet, printed on both sides. (Available from any local printer/high-street print shop, at approx £100/150 per thousand, plus about £50 for layout.)
2. Headline it with something like: '5 Nasty Household Jobs I Can Do For You! Call me today on 22200', or 'Frank's Friendly Plumbing Service – call 7766 any time', or 'Sam's Quality Painting Service – call 9944 for a free quote'.
3. Explain how customers will benefit from your service; then if possible, quote other satisfied customers; finally, give details of your guarantee/after-sales service.
4. Carry a stock of these leaflets in your van. Give one to all your new customers and/or pop them through letter-boxes. Result? Your written sales message will help you to sell more!

Conclusion – the written word works!

Not very long ago, I visited a lady aromatherapist to buy a series of beauty treatments as a birthday present for my wife. Our conversation went something like this:

Me: Good morning. I'd like to buy a few treatments for my wife. Could you give me a brochure or something, so I can see the sort of things you do?

Her: I'm sorry, I don't have a brochure.

Me: Oh. Er . . . do you give vouchers then?
Her: I'm afraid not.
Me: OK, er . . . could you *tell* me what you do?
Her: I'm sorry, I'm actually with a client at the moment.
Me: Goodbye. (What else could I say?)

The moral? Start putting your sales message on paper!

For advice on how to mailshot business customers with your sales literature, see page 73.

5

How to turn enquiries into sales

How not to handle a phone enquiry

Caller:	Is that Nellie's Garden Centre?
Nellie:	Yes, it is.
Caller:	Do you sell garden furniture?
Nellie:	Yes, we do.
Caller:	Fine, I'll call in sometime. Thanks.

To find out what Nellie should have done, read on.

The 5 Finger Method of handling enquiries

Whenever someone rings (or visits) you with an enquiry, you should do five things: one for each finger on your hand.

1. *Make the customer feel good about calling you.*
    Thank him for ringing. Ask how he found out about you.

2. *Ask how you can help now or in the future.*
    Ask exactly what he wants, but don't stop there! Ask if he needs anything else.

3. *Tell him how you can help.*
    Once you know what he wants, tell him what you have that will solve his problem and give him the result he is looking for.

4. *Always suggest a course of action.*
   Never hang up before suggesting (a) he gives you an order there and then, ie, to stop him going elsewhere; or (b) he visits you (or you visit him) to talk more; or (c) he waits to hear from you, before proceeding, ie, to allow you time to check up on things. *Tip: Help him to buy by having some specific offers ready!*

5. *Always ask the customer for his name and address/phone number.*
   Never let a customer hang up before you get his details. If you do, you may lose a source of valuable future sales.

Five ways to make life easier for yourself

1. *Keep a writing pad and pen next to the phone.*
   If this sounds too obvious to be worth mentioning, think how many times you have said to a customer 'Hold on while I find a pen'. If necessary, chain a pad and pen to the nearest wall.

2. *Keep a list of key questions on the cover of your pad.*
   We all forget things in the heat of the moment. However, forgetting, for example, to ask a customer for his name and address may cost you money, so keep a list of relevant questions to hand.

3. *Keep important product information handy.*
   If your customers usually need specific information about your product, keep it handy. If necessary, make a separate set of this sort of information and keep it next to the phone.

4. *Train your partner/employees to answer the phone properly.*
   A customer will always judge you (and your firm) by the way you answer his enquiry. Make sure that whoever answers the phone knows the 5 Finger Method.

5. *Check what your local computer store can offer you.*
   For about £1400 (see page 125) you can buy a small computer system with printer and relevant software. Here's how this sort of technology can help you and your business:

- **You can write letters/quotations faster!**
  Make a mistake? Zip! It's gone. Want to change words or move a paragraph? Zip! It's done. You'll never use another typewriter!
- **You can store (and recall) customer details faster!**
  Want to find out who bought what, when, at what price from you, last year? Zip! You get the answer immediately.
- **You can write standard letters/quotations/price lists faster!**
  Need a new price list? Need to write your 53rd quotation? Want to send out a standard letter to all your customers? It's easy with a computer. But don't take my word for it. Ask for a demo at your local store. If you don't, your competitors might beat you to it.

How to make the most of every enquiry

The 5 Finger Method is a simple way of getting the most out of every inquiry. Here are some examples of how to adapt this method to various different business situations.

Gertrude runs a dog kennels. Whenever someone rings up to enquire about her service, she always makes a point of thanking them and being as friendly as possible. She knows that if she comes across as a kindly individual, the caller will feel reassured about entrusting her with his precious pet. **Result:** she turns nearly all her enquiries into sales.

Cleopatra owns Cool-Heads Ltd – a small employment agency that provides full-time and temp secretaries for company directors. Whenever she receives an enquiry, she asks lots of questions about what the company does and how it is run. This helps her to gauge how to sell her service to the customer. It also generates other bits of valuable information, for example the names of other directors (each of whom might need a secretary, at some stage). **Result?** From each enquiry, Cleopatra usually gets four up-to-date names. After six months, she has a list of 300 directors, all of whom duly receive her brochure.

Silas has a small farm. To supplement his income, he sells a range of products to the general public, including fresh eggs, frozen meat, free-range chickens, manure, fresh fruits (strawberries, gooseberries etc) and potatoes. Whenever someone enquires about one particular product (eg, eggs), he also tells them about all his other products. **Result?** No one buys just one thing from Silas.

Chuck owns a small distribution business, selling fruit and veg to a range of corner shops and small grocers. What his customers need is fast service and good quality produce. In order to demonstrate to all enquirers how effectively he meets these needs, he adopts the following approach:

- He tells them that he is the most expensive distributor in the area;
- He explains why – because he's the best: ie, he gives the fastest service and offers the best produce.

Most customers believe him, thinking: if he charges more than other distributors, he must be the best! **Result?** Chuck's blunt confidence in his service enables him to turn most of his enquiries into firm sales.

Lucy runs a small au pair agency. Whenever someone rings to enquire about her service, she nearly always uses it as an excuse to visit their house. **Result?** She is able to meet her customers face to face in the intimacy of their home, and give them a thorough presentation of how she can help.

Karl is a self-employed furniture restorer. He receives lots of enquiries from people whose sole concern seems to be price; ie, how much does he charge? As it happens, he is finding that his prices are being severely undercut by New Age competitors who lack his skills but charge less. His solution is to avoid quoting a price until he has seen and discussed the piece of furniture with the customer, preferably at the customer's house. **Result?** When customers see and hear him talk about their furniture, they recognise that his skills are worth paying for.

Crispin owns a toy shop. Next to the counter he has a brightly coloured box labelled *'Free Raffle – Big Prizes!'* Whenever a customer calls, he points to the box and suggests they enter. All they have to do is write their name, address and what they are looking for in the shop, on a slip of paper. In return, they might win a nice toy – and if they don't collect it, he'll give it to a local orphanage. Most customers enter, the bulk of them, kids. **Result?** By 1 September each year, he usually has about 1000 up-to-date names and addresses. He then sends each person a copy of his Christmas catalogue and a £5 voucher redeemable against all orders of £25 or more. Then, on 27 December, he sends out a letter (plus voucher) – this time to kids only, to help them spend their Xmas money.

Conan owns a small firm that builds and paves new driveways. Every time he has an enquiry he takes the customer's details and gives him a quotation. If, after a month, the customer has still not given him the go ahead, he drives past the customer's address to see if the job has gone to someone else. Those who have not had a new drive laid, he recontacts to find out whether they wish to go ahead with his quote after all. **Result?** Not only does he follow up on all enquiries, he also finds out what type of drive his customers prefer and who they get to build it. He can thus improve his service accordingly.

Grant is a dynamic young businessman with his own mobile disco. Whenever the owner of a pub or club rings about his service, Grant takes his details and writes them into his Filofax. Then, whether or not the owner offers him work there and then, he keeps in touch. After two years, his Filofax is crammed with the names of customers throughout his locality. **Result?** Whenever they need a DJ, the first person they think of is Grant.

As Grant himself puts it – 'know a million people, make a million pounds'.

'Mountie' Mick has a small plumbing business. Whenever someone rings to ask him to quote for a job, he records their details in a file. Then, whether or not his quote is accepted, he faithfully recontacts each customer (every eight weeks) to ask whether they need anything doing. **Result?** Over time, he converts nearly 75 per cent of all his enquiries into sales. What's more, because of his helpful manner, many of these 75 per cent recommend him to their friends, which more than compensates him for the 25 per cent who offer him nothing. Now you know why he is called Mountie Mick: he always gets his customer!

Flossie is a self-employed photographer. She tries to get referrals from her customers. When they ring, she tells them that nearly all her business comes through personal recommendation. Then, she asks whether they know anyone else who might want to use her service. **Result?** Her reference to personal recommendation not only reassures callers about buying, it also encourages them to offer referrals. On average, from every six enquiries, Flossie receives one referral and so boosts her potential customers by 16 per cent!

Checklist

• **Use the 5 Finger Method to answer all enquiries.**

1. Make the customer feel good.
2. Ask how you can help.
3. Tell him how you can help.
4. Always suggest a course of action.
5. *Always get the customer's name/address/phone number!*

NB: If you employ someone else to answer enquiries, make sure that they know the 5 Finger Method!

6

Start offering customers what they really want!

Do you know what your customers really want? Are you doing your best to satisfy them? If you're not, you're losing money!

How *not* to satisfy customers – some classic examples

Larry owns a garage that services and repairs cars. One busy Friday afternoon, a customer turns up with a car whose engine is badly misfiring. Larry tells the customer 'Sorry mate, we're too busy. Leave the car here if you want, but it won't get looked at until Monday morning at the earliest.' **Result?** Larry loses a customer for life.

Larry's mistake: First, like any garage-owner, Larry should know that car-drivers get desperate when things go wrong with their cars! So, if Friday is a peak time, he should organise extra staff to cope with the increased demand and, if possible, he should also offer a Saturday service. Also, even if he *is* fully booked, he should at least spend a few minutes on the customer's problem. By doing this, he is bound to increase his chances of getting the customer's future business.

Deirdre owns a small mail-order company. She sells sweatshirts imprinted with various humorous messages. The small print of her catalogue states: if a customer orders an item that is out of stock she reserves the right to substitute a similar item. One day, a customer orders (and sends a cheque for) a short-sleeved sweatshirt imprinted with message No 7. Deirdre has run out of short-sleeved No 7s and so sends a long-sleeved one instead. **Result?** She loses a customer for life.

Deirdre's mistake: Mail-order customers trust suppliers to act fairly. Deirdre should either have returned the cheque or given the customer the option of another style/design of sweatshirt. For the sake of a few pounds she has lost all chance of future business – not just from the customer but probably from the customer's friends as well.

Butch owns a TV/video rental shop. His two telephone lines are almost always engaged. This makes it very difficult for customers to contact him and very frustrating for anyone whose TV or video has stopped working. **Result?** He loses business to a local rival who is easier to contact.

Butch's mistake: Offering a service that he cannot support.

Lavinia owns a ladies hairdressers. She has an excellent taste and generally knows what hairstyle is best for each customer. She therefore tends to ignore what customers actually want and instead gives them the style that (in her opinion) looks best. **Result?** She loses customers!

Lavinia's mistake: She forgets that her job is to offer customers what they want – not what is good for them.

Benito owns an Italian restaurant. One day, a customer asks for egg and chips. Benito explains that egg and chips is not on the menu. **Result?** He loses a customer for life.

Benito's mistake: He forgets that some customers are different. The least he should do, before declining the customer's request, is to check with his chef to see whether it is possible.

How <u>not</u> to sell to customers in the home – a classic example

Mr and Mrs Homeowner decide to hire a builder to convert their lounge and dining room into one big room. Although they have no exact idea of what's involved or how much the job will cost, they *do* have four basic concerns: (a) they want a reliable job done; (b) they don't want to be ripped off; (c) they want the minimum amount of mess; and (d) they want the builder to turn up on time.

Because they have never used a builder before, they consult the *Yellow Pages* and speak to three small building firms who each agree to visit the house and offer a quote. Although they each arrive separately, they all take a similar approach:

- They each spend a few moments talking to Mr Homeowner to find out what he wants doing.
- They inspect the walls, take measurements and ask one or two more questions; eg, when is the job to be done? None of them make any attempt at polite conversation during this process.
- Finally, after saying something like: 'Well, I think I've got everything I need', they each tell Mr Homeowner that they will contact him with a definite price within a day or so, and then leave.

The builders' mistakes:

- *None of them take any real interest in the concerns of the Homeowners.* Instead, each of them treats the whole thing as if it is a simple mathematical exercise; ie, just a matter of calculating how much materials/labour is needed.
- *None of them make any attempt to introduce themselves properly or to demonstrate that their skills and service are worth buying.* For example, none of them bother to show Mr Homeowner any recommendations from other satisfied customers or bother to discuss the job with him, to overcome any worries he may have.

- *None of them discuss cost, or offer an approximate quote.* As a result, Mr Homeowner is left in limbo and none the wiser for their visit.

The correct approach

Homeowners need information and reassurance. Give it to them!

- Introduce yourself properly. Offer a business card.
- Ask the customer what he wants; discuss what needs to be done.
- Take the trouble to explain the likely problems and how you intend to handle them. Show the customer your testimonials from other satisfied customers.
- Find out what he wants to spend. Ask whether he would like an idea of how much the job will cost; if so, give it to him.
- Above all, make the customer feel *comfortable* with you. Remember: very few customers buy from people they don't feel comfortable with.

How to give customers what they *really* want

Make it more convenient for customers to buy from you

No matter what sort of firm you have, you can always make it easier for customers to do business with you. For example:

Marie-Antoinette owns a cake shop. To make it easier for less mobile senior citizens to buy their favourite cakes and to help busy parents buy birthday cakes for their kids, she introduces a dial-a-cake service for all orders of £15 or more. She advertises by direct mail to all local retirement homes, and all local firms. **Result?** Her sales go up. (Surprisingly, her biggest sales are to offices celebrating staff birthdays.)

Len is a butcher, like his father before him. Six months ago, a new supermarket opened nearby. As a result, Len's trade is suffering. Len knows that one reason for this is because the supermarket makes it easy for customers to help themselves to the meat they want. Despite this, he doesn't offer any sort of self-service. Why not? Because he never has! **Result?** His sales continue to shrink.

Basil owns a mobile food business selling sandwiches to workers in suburban industrial estates. For several months he enjoys a complete monopoly. As a result, he gets lazy: he doesn't always show up on time and occasionally doesn't bother turning up at all. Gradually, his customers become more and more irritated – they need a supplier whom they can rely on to be at a certain place at a certain time. If not, they go hungry! Then another mobile food-seller – *Nifty Ned* – moves into the area. Unlike Basil, Ned knows that what customers really want is reliable service, so he always turns up on time. **Result?** Most of Basil's customers start buying from Ned.

Wayne is a plumber. Every time he visits someone to repair their washing machine etc, he asks them whether – 'just to be on the safe side' – they want him to check anything else (dishwasher, radiators, tank, boiler, outside pipes etc). **Result?** By making it easy for customers to use his service, he makes maximum use of every call and more money into the bargain.

Guy is also a plumber. He has another trick. Whenever he repairs a domestic boiler or washing machine or tumble dryer etc, he sticks a small label on it. It reads: 'For future repair or service, contact Guy on 444 222'. **Result?** Next time the appliance breaks down, the owner knows exactly who to contact and how.

Cinderella and *Alphonse* have a Sunday market stall where they sell their own hand-made pullovers, priced at £45 upwards. At first, sales are very low, then Cinders (the brains of the operation) has an idea. She realises that they are not making it easy for customers to buy because they have nothing to offer anyone with less than £45 to spend. She therefore decides to make a range of cheap, easy to knit, brightly coloured woollen scarves and hats for kids, priced at £2.99 upwards. **Result?** Not only do the scarves and hats sell like hot cakes, but as customers stop to buy these items they also buy some pullovers as well.

Marion runs a slimming class in a local town. Because she knows that many slimmers prefer to lose weight in private, she decides to offer private consultations in her home. **Result?** Her business expands as more slimmers take advantage of her service.

Take calculated risks to give customers what they really want

For example, when my partner and I started our first business, we decided to offer all customers free overnight delivery. At the time this was considered a waste of money by most of our competitors who were content to offer (at best) 48-hour delivery. In addition, in order to guarantee early arrival of brand new products, we sometimes paid cash on delivery to our suppliers. This, too, was considered unnecessary by our rivals. But *fast delivery of brand new products was exactly what our customers wanted.* As a result, little else was needed to persuade them to switch their business to our company.

Here are some more examples of how to take a calculated risk:

Jacko has his own car repair/servicing company. He knows that most people who want their car serviced hate the inconvenience of driving their car to the garage in the morning and picking it up again in the evening. He therefore takes a risk and offers a special pick-up-and-return-service for all customers who want their cars serviced.

The service costs him a total of £120 a day in extra wages.

However, he charges each customer a small extra fee for the service, which reduces the cost to about £60 a day; ie, roughly the price of one car-service. **Result?** Within three months, Jacko is servicing five extra cars a day, his future bookings look even better and his customers have never been happier!

Theo owns a travel agency. He knows that many of his customers are wary of booking holidays in foreign resorts which they know nothing about. To help remedy this, he takes a risk and buys a wide range of videos, featuring various countries and resorts in the Mediterranean area. Over the next 12 months, using various different sources (including home-made film), he adds to his collection until he has videos on nearly every major tourist spot in the Mediterranean. He then edits them into 10 minute sections for easy viewing in his office. **Result?** For an investment of about £3000, Theo creates a unique customer service which gradually turns his travel agency into one of the best in the locality.

Bob and *Madonna* make a range of beautiful hand-painted crockery from their workshop located in the wilds of Shropshire. Alas, despite their obvious skills, sales are low and neither can afford to give up their full-time jobs. One reason for their lack of commercial success is price – at a retail price of £24 per plate, their crockery is a high-risk purchase. Many shops are worried about buying it in case they are left with unsold stock. After careful thought, Bob and Madonna decide to take a risk in order to give their retail customers exactly what they want. First, they invest £3000 in making several complete ranges of their most spectacular crockery. Second, using a copy of *Newman's Retail Directory* (see page 71), they make appointments to see the buyers for six large London stores. Finally, after presenting samples of their crockery, they offer each buyer 100 per cent sale-or-return on all first orders. Faced with an offer they can't reasonably refuse, four out of six buyers place orders. Within a month, Bob and Madonna's products are seen by customers in four top locations. **Result?** One store sells out and places two further orders that pay for the whole sale-or-return experiment.

Over the next 12 months, further UK and overseas orders give Bob and Madonna the commercial breakthrough they need. They never look back.

Don't be afraid to change – listen to what customers tell you

Dougal owns a toyshop. Every January he gets lots of telephone calls from people with broken toys. After a couple of years he finally gets the message and decides to offer a toy-repair service. (Amazingly, after ringing up several of his competitors, he discovers that no other toy shop offers this kind of service.) To help him do this, he rings up several carpenters/handymen until he finds two suitable candidates. He then advertises the new service with a large bold notice in his shop window. **Result?** Almost immediately, more customers come into his shop. After three months, Dougal decides to expand further by offering second-hand toys for sale – another unique service not offered by his rivals. He now offers most customers what they really want: new full-price toys, second-hand cheaper toys and a repair service!

Zebedee is a landscape gardener and has qualifications to prove it. Unfortunately, sales are down. One day in April, he reads a gardening article in his local newspaper which gives advice to gardeners on how to minimise back pain when weeding. This gives him an idea. He jumps into his car and spends an hour driving around his local suburb, inspecting people's driveways and front gardens. Many are covered in weeds. The next day, Zebedee orders 1000 leaflets which he immediately delivers to local houses. The leaflet is headlined: 'Does your garden or driveway need weeding? Does your lawn need cutting? Does your garden need tidying up? Don't delay – contact Zebedee on 666555'. **Result?** Although only a few people need the services of a professional landscaper, a huge number want someone to do the simpler jobs of weeding and grass-cutting. Zebedee's sales boom!

Checklist

Ask yourself these questions:

1. Do you regularly ask your customers how your service might be improved?
2. Do you regularly ask your friends or other business acquaintances how your service might be improved?
3. Do you ever ask those customers who refuse to buy from you, why they don't?

If you don't, you should!

7

Ten easy ways to find new customers

1. Draw up a list of companies/individuals to sell to

Go into the reference section of your local main library. Ask to see the following reference publications:

- *The (UK) Kompass Directory:* This lists all the larger UK firms and tells you what they do and where they do it. Very useful if you want to sell something to a particular type of company.
- *Newman's Retail Directory:* This lists the buyers of several thousand retail stores – large and small. A vital reference if you want to sell to the retail trade.
- *Local company register:* This lists all local companies.
- *Yellow Pages:* Always a useful reference.

Buying a ready-made list

It's cheaper to do your own research and make your own list but if you want to buy a ready-made list of companies and/or individuals, contact a list broker (ie, a firm that sells lists). To find a list broker contact the *Direct Marketing Association (DMA) UK Ltd,* Haymarket House, 1 Oxendon Street, London SW1Y 4EE; Tel: 0171 321 2525.

Alternatively, give these four companies a call. Each has different expertise to offer and *all* are worth investigating.

- *Business Lists UK Ltd,* 4 Gillbent Road, Cheadle Hulme, Cheshire SK8 6NB; Tel: 0161 488 4166.
- *Dudley & Jenkins plc*, 2a Southwark Bridge Office Village, Thrale Street, London SE1 9JG; Tel: 0171 407 5987 Fax: 0171 407 6294.
- *Dun's Marketing*, Dun & Bradstreet, Holmers Farm Way, High Wycombe, Bucks HP12 4UL; Tel: 01494 422299 Fax: 01494 423698.
- *Yellow Pages,* Tel: 0800 600900.

What sort of ready-made lists can you buy?

- Lists of specific companies (ie, companies defined by the type of products they make/distribute/retail or by the type of service they offer).
- Lists of specific companies defined by geographic location.
- Lists of key individuals defined by job status, by earnings, or by lifestyle (NB: These lists include home address.)
- Any other list capable of being compiled by reference to information that is publicly available.

How big a list can you buy?

Lists are sold *per thousand names.* Thereafter, you are only limited by what you can afford. For example, today's commercial databases contain up-to-date information on over 1.5 million large and medium-sized firms throughout the UK.

What details does a typical list include?

There is no such thing as a 'typical list' – all lists vary. However, most *company* lists include a minimum of:

- Company name.
- Type of business.
- One or more executive names (eg, MD/finance director etc).
- Company address, phone number, fax number.
- Other information as requested (turnover/no of employees/financial status etc).

Lists of *individuals* can vary more widely. They can include:

• Name of individual.
• Home address, phone number.
• Gender.
• Job status.
• Lifestyle interest.
• Other information, as requested.

NB: Most lists are guaranteed 95 per cent accurate and are available on disc, label or printout.

How much does a typical list cost?

As a general rule of thumb, the more information you want your list to have, the more it will cost. (Discs and labels sometimes cost extra.)

As a very rough guide, expect to pay between £80 and £130 per thousand names for a fairly standard list; between £130 and £200 (or more) for something more detailed.

Tip: Certain trade associations will allow you to rent their membership list. Such a list may be cheaper and slightly more up to date than a commercially available one. To find out what trade associations exist, ask your librarian for a copy of the Directory of British Associations. Then write to the Secretary of the relevant association – remembering to stress how reliable your firm is, and how your product will be of interest to the members of the association.

2. Use mailshots to contact new business customers

Before you do anything, ring the Post Office

Contact your local Royal Mail Account Manager and ask for details on *Mailsort*. This is a special service for companies who mail out large quantities of letters/packets: (eg, 4000 letters or

1000 packets, or 2000 letters posted and delivered in the same postal district). It offers discounts of between 13 and 32 per cent on normal postage rates. Call free on 0800 378671 for details.

How to get the most from your mailshot

Don't mailshot without thinking! Follow these nine steps:

1. *Prepare/acquire a suitable list of companies.*
   — Ideally the list should contain at least 100 companies.
   — Make sure the list includes phone numbers for all firms.
2. *Telephone each company for the name of the relevant buyer.*
   — Get a specific name to send your mailshot to. By ringing first, you also find out if the firm has moved!
   — Address each envelope to the relevant buyer.
   — If your list already has these names, so much the better.
3. *Speak to each buyer, to establish interest.*
   — Introduce yourself and your firm.
   — Get some general information about the buyer's priorities.
   — Unless the buyer genuinely resists, explain that you will be mailing him written details about your product.
4. *Decide what you want to send to each buyer.*
   — Re-read Chapter 4 for what to put in your sales literature.
   — If sending a sales brochure, remember to include a covering letter and add a PS. (Everyone reads covering letters/PS's!)
   — Use self-adhesive envelopes – they save you lots of time!
5. *Post off 40 copies of your mailshot (unless using Mailsort)*
   — Why? Because each recipient of your mailshot should receive a follow-up phone call from you, within 48 hours, while it is still fresh in his mind. If you send out more, many recipients will have forgotten about it by the time you call.
   — Always use second class postage.

6. *Follow up each envelope with a phone call to its recipient.*
   — Allow 48 hours for delivery, then phone.
   — When doing this use a telesales script (see page 114).
7. *Try to get something from each customer.*
   — Get him to buy (re-read Chapters 1–3); or
   — Get him to think about it and arrange to call him back; or
   — Get him to discuss the matter again (eg in one month's time); or
   — Get him to make an appointment for you to see him.
8. *Keep a record of all your telephone calls.*
   — Ideally, keep a separate record card on each customer.
   — Erase from your list all customers who have moved, or who are genuinely uninterested in your product.
9. *Repeat the phone/post/phone sequence until all copies sent.*
   — Never simply post off a sales brochure without following it up with a phone call – you will waste money.

3. Make the most of your own business records

Dig out the names and addresses of all those customers who contacted you for information (over the past 12 months) but didn't order anything.

Monty runs a small firm of office cleaners. One day, in an effort to generate more sales, he sorts through his files and makes a list of all the companies to whom he sent his brochure during the previous year, but who didn't buy. The total is 278. Over the next fortnight, he rings them all – starting with the more recent ones first. **Result?**

- 48 have moved or else have been disconnected;
- 80 won't speak to him;
- 40 are 'not interested': they do not need cleaners;
- 60 ask for another brochure but without much enthusiasm;

- 20 ask for another brochure and are 'interested';
- 20 make an appointment for him to see them;
- 10 immediately hire his service, starting the following week.

From the 'interested' group, and from his appointments, he makes a further 17 sales; making a total of 27 new sales from 278 files gathering dust.

4. Ask yourself: 'Who else can use my product or service?'

Try to think of different types of customer who might have a use for your product. Ideally, discuss the matter with a friend whose outlook is different from yours.

Napoleon owns a small travel agency. In order to appeal to additional types of customer, he decides to offer a range of special-interest holidays. First, he makes contact with a number of local groups (eg, garage-owners, chess-players, schools etc) to test demand and to find out what each group might be interested in. Then, he contacts his local airline and puts together eight special trips: two to see a pair of Formula One Grand Prix's, two to see a pair of European chess events, and four off-season trips for sixth-formers. His research pays off: nearly all the trips are fully booked. **Result?** His sales go up. Next year, he plans extra trips to an international stamp fair, a German bird-sanctuary and a tour of WWl battlefields.

Justin is a self-employed photographer. About 60 per cent of his work comes from design studios and advertising agencies; the rest comes from private customers. Because business is slow, Justin tries to think of different customers to sell to. Eventually, he hits upon an idea: why not sell his service to estate agents – after all, they need lots of houses photographed. He gets to work. First, he has a chat with an estate agent friend of his and learns that competition for photographic work is fierce. Undaunted, he puts together a portfolio of his previous work together with an impressive folder of testimonials from satisfied customers. Then, armed with this sales material, he makes appointments to see the 12 largest estate agents in the area. **Result?** One of them gives him a full-time commission, worth £80 a week for two years. His idea has boosted his sales by 25 per cent!

Shark-Face Sam owns a tropical fish shop. One day he reads about a New York law firm that has a tropical aquarium in its waiting room, to relax its clients. If it works in New York, thinks Sam, why not over here? He gets on to it straight away. First, he visits his local library and asks to see their local company register. From this, he makes a list of 100 local firms with more than 30 employees, ie, firms who are more likely to have proper reception facilities.

Next, over a period of 8 weeks, he visits each firm to check the size of their reception area, to find out who is responsible for buying something like tropical fish tanks and to hand over a copy of his brochure. Finally, he phones each buyer to determine interest. **Result?** Amazingly, the third person he calls – the MD of a medium-sized company – asks him to call in and explain what he offers. He does so and the MD gives him an order for £600. Not a bad start for a new idea!

5. Be smart – take your product to the customer

Jimmy owns a small building firm. He knows that people who have just moved house often want to make alterations to their new home. So, every weekend he (and his two partners) drive around their respective areas, looking for 'Sold' signs outside houses for sale. Every time they see one they note down the address. Then, a month later one of them calls to the house, gives the new owners his business card, briefly explains his expertise and asks them to ring him if they decide to do any alterations. **Result?** By taking their product to the customer, Jimmy and his partners get about 40 new customers a year.

Adam is a self-employed carpenter. Throughout the year (but especially during the winter months) he keeps an eye on the weather. When severe winds are forecast, he organises a series of leaflet drops to houses in the suburbs. The leaflet is headlined 'Emergency Fence Repair! For immediate action, telephone Adam on 234 5678'. **Result?** By taking his service to the customer (instead of waiting for the customer to choose his name – or not – out of the *Yellow Pages*), Adam keeps ahead of the competition.

Ben owns a small firm that repairs and services cars. Like Adam, Ben also watches the weather. When cold winter weather is forecast, he pops his own leaflet through local letter-boxes. One side of the leaflet explains his 'Early Morning Flat Battery Service' (flat batteries recharged from 6am onwards); the other explains his '15 Minute Anti-freeze Service' (customers who bring their cars to his garage can have anti-freeze put in within 15 minutes). **Result?** Ben sells to more new customers.

Cher owns a small firm which offers secretarial services to small companies and private individuals. Her scheme for contacting customers goes like this. First, she orders 200 luminous A5-size cards from her local printer – these are headlined 'Need Your Thesis Typed? – For fast action, ring Cher on 987 6543!' Second, she visits all her local colleges (plus their student halls of residence, their other student hostels, and their Student Union offices) and pins up her cards on all relevant notice boards. **Result?** Her luminous cards are seen by a large proportion of students who need their theses typed.

Lenny is an ambitious 21 year old who intends to become a millionaire. He already owns a small firm (himself plus two young employees) which produces a range of videos including Tai chi, cooking, plant-care, palmistry, card tricks etc. They are sold mainly by mail-order but also through local retail outlets. His new customer campaign goes like this:

First, he puts together a short business plan, describing his business and showing how much he intends to sell, to whom, over the next 12 months. Armed with this plan, he visits his bank manager to negotiate a loan, which he uses to pay for a printed colour brochure, better coloured packaging for his videos plus some new luminous point-of-sale stickers to attract shopper attention. The brochure makes his firm appear a lot more established than it really is, while the videos' new packaging gives them a look of real quality.

Next, he visits his local library and consults *Newman's Retail Directory*, from which he makes a list of 62 named individuals who buy video products for all the major chain-stores. He then rings them all up, arranges to send each of them a copy of his brochure and makes 25 appointments to present his case. In order to prepare for these appointments, he types a detailed explanation of each video. He also makes a small file of testimonials from satisfied retail customers. Then, he thinks up 10 difficult questions that he may be asked and tries to work out answers to each: he role-plays them all with a friend. Then, armed with a case of video samples and a range of point-of-sale stickers, he visits each buyer as arranged. **Result?** He gets one medium order and five small orders. In addition, after agreeing to 50 per cent sale or return with the buyers for four large London department stores, he receives two more medium-sized orders.

Finally, he recontacts the other 37 buyers who were unable to make an appointment for him to see them. Over the next three months, he sees all but 12. This nets him more orders and more contacts. **Result?** Lenny's attention to detail and (above all) his willingness to take his products to his customers, gives him a solid base of new customers.

Manfred is a freelance photographer. Because business is slack, he decides to take his service direct to the customer. First, he consults his local *Yellow Pages* and makes a list of all builders, painters and decorators. Next he rings them all up and offers to help each of them make more money. The idea is this: he will provide *before* and *after* photos of each job they do. By having photos taken of (say) five or six jobs, they will have an impressive file of evidence with which to impress their new customers and win more orders. **Result?** From 100 telephone conversations, he makes 40 appointments which result in 18 sales. What's more, six of these 18 customers are so pleased with Manfred's work that they give him a regular monthly contract. They also recommend him to their friends in other trades, which results in four other regular contracts.

The moral? Don't wait for customers to contact you: go out and contact them!

6. Sell to flagship customers to make a name for yourself

One of the problems of running a small business is that most people have never heard of you! One way to overcome this is to choose a well-known customer and make him an offer he can't reasonably refuse.

Then, use the fact that your product is now used by this big name, to promote yourself to other firms. After all, these firms will think: 'If it's good enough for a big name, it's good enough for us.'

For example, when my partner and I started our business, we made offers to several large London stores and one major chain-store, which they couldn't reasonably refuse. This enabled us to tell all other retailers that our firm supplied 'several major UK retailers' – enough to give us instant credibility in the eyes of other retailers and a definite edge over our competitors. Here are some more examples:

Billy is a young self-employed accountant. In order to overcome his relative anonymity, he signs an agreement with the Small Farmers Association to provide their members with a fixed-price accountancy service. **Result?** Although his charge for this service is only half his normal rate, being able to write 'accountant to the Small Farms Association' on his business stationery gives him instant credibility in the eyes of new customers.

Frances runs a firm that makes novelty corkscrews in the shape of politicians' heads. In order to impress other retailers she offers them to Harrods and Selfridges at 100 per cent sale or return. Both agree. **Result?** Frances immediately tells all her new customers that she supplies several famous London stores: they are suitably impressed.

Virginia owns a small firm that makes Squish – a low-cost yogurt. To boost her sales she approaches the local branch managers of three national supermarkets and asks them to allow her to offer free tastings to their customers, one day a week. At the same time, she offers to supply them with a range of Squish at 100 per cent sale or return. After vetting her production methods and hygiene, one of the managers agrees. **Result?** Her free tastings help her yogurts to sell out. The supermarket manager is impressed. Meanwhile, Virginia's telesales staff are telling all other retailers in the country that Squish yogurts are so good that they are now stocked by a major supermarket. Sales go up.

> *Tip: Only make irresistible offers after you have made a proper sales presentation: never use large discounts or sale-or-return as a substitute for selling your product on its merits.*

7. Make joint arrangements with another small firm

Another simple way of finding new customers is to swop skills and/or information with another small firm. For example:

Chip owns a hardware shop. He teams up with *Dan*, a painter and decorator. Chip puts up a notice next to his counter saying

'Need any painting done? Why not use our own professional painting and decorating service? Ask for a free quote, today!' **Result?** By combining in this way, both are better off. Dan gets more work and Chip (who gets 10 per cent of the profits) makes more money.

Sybil owns a guest house in the Lake District. She teams up with two different people. The first is *Mao-Mao*, who owns a local restaurant. In return for booking meals for her guests at his restaurant, Mao-Mao gives her five per cent of what they spend. The second is *Katarina*, who owns another guest house 10 miles further along the tourist route. Sybil and Katarina recommend each other's accommodation and offer all guests a special discount if they stay at both guest houses. By pooling resources in this way, both are better off.

Spanner Jack repairs lawnmowers. He teams up with *Fergal*, who owns a garden nursery. Fergal advertises Jack's service and they split the profits. **Result?** By combining, both get more new customers than they would on their own.

> *Tip: Don't be put off by the fact that this type of arrangement requires a certain amount of organisation. However, to avoid any misunderstandings, make a point of putting the arrangement on paper, so that both of you know exactly what the deal is.*

8. Expand your contacts!

If you run a small business that no one has heard of, you must learn to promote yourself whenever and wherever you can.

Buy yourself some business cards

- Go into any high street print-shop and ask for a mid-price type of business card. Don't get anything too expensive, but avoid anything that looks too cheap!

- Order as many as you can afford – I suggest a minimum of 300. The price per card drops significantly the more you order.
- Make your business name self-explanatory. For example, a card which reads 'F. Bloggs Ltd' is unhelpful because it doesn't say what F. Bloggs Ltd *does!* Much better is 'F. Bloggs Ltd (Translation Services).'
- At the foot of your card, put a one-line message to draw the reader's attention to an aspect of your product. For example, F. Bloggs' card reads 'Specialists in all European languages'.

Carry your business cards everywhere and give them out

Edna and *Madge* run a small jam-making business. Most of their sales are to local shops and supermarkets, although they also supply private customers. To boost their private customer sales, both of them always carry a supply of business cards in their handbags and give them out to anyone who sounds in the least bit interested in home-made jam. Edna's speciality is handing them out at the hairdressers and at local Conservative Party events, while Madge hands them out to anyone she chats to in the local pub and at meetings of the local Women's Institute. **Result?** Everyone knows that Edna and Madge sell home-made jam!

Get to know useful people

Start meeting people who can help further your business – people who might buy from you, or give you information, or help you to promote your business, or introduce you to others who might do all or any of these things. For example:

- *Join your national/local trade association.*
  Membership usually offers you a variety of benefits such as extra credibility in the eyes of customers; inclusion in the Association's *Yellow Pages* advertising; subsidised technical

or legal advice; information on suppliers; special discounts etc. To contact your particular association, ask your main librarian for a copy of the *Directory of British Associations*.

- *Join your local Chamber of Commerce.*
  By doing this, you will meet a wide variety of different business people, each with their own ideas and contacts to share with you: which accountant to use, which journalist to contact on the local paper, which bank manager is most sympathetic to small firms and so on.

- *Contact your local university/college Students Union.*
  They can often provide useful information (eg, lists of local landlords, lists of students looking for temporary work etc); help you to arrange demonstrations of your product, or find people to deliver leaflets etc.

- *Contact local schools/colleges/Women's Institute etc.*
  If your product is suitable, arrange demonstrations or displays.

  Tip: When telling someone what you do, make it sound more interesting by explaining how you help people!

One of the best salesmen I ever knew used to sell insurance in London on a commission basis only. This meant that if he didn't sell anything, he didn't earn anything. One of his favourite methods of finding new customers was to go to a smart pub after work and simply strike up conversation with strangers. When he was asked what he did for a living (as he usually was), he would say: 'I arrange mortgages for people' – which was perfectly true, except every mortgage was sold with a life assurance policy which was what paid his commission. As he explained this, he would always hand the listener his business card. **Result?** According to him, 1 in 12 of his listeners would end up buying an insurance policy from him. Imagine how different their reaction would have been if he had said 'I sell life assurance!'

9. Use magazines!

Consumer magazines

If you sell to the retail trade, a quick way of finding new customers is to buy some consumer magazines that contain large advertisements for products that are likely to be stocked by the sort of shop you want to sell to. Why do this? Because many such advertisements contain a list of shops from whom the reader may obtain the advertised product.

When my partner and I started selling computer software, we scoured every computer magazine we could find, for advertisements containing the names/addresses/telephone numbers of computer shops. After eight weeks we had a list of 350 shops, each of whom we telephoned and then mailed with our product list. **Result?** We generated a huge number of new customers without spending a penny on advertising.

Trade magazines are also useful

- If you want to find out about companies who operate in a particular industry, consult the relevant trade magazine. As well as telling you who does what in the industry, trade magazines will tell you what trade shows are imminent and so on.
- Many trade magazines also publish a yearbook, containing a comprehensive list of all firms who operate within the industry. To obtain a free copy, say you are thinking of advertising in the next edition and ask to seek the current one.
- Start by asking your local librarian for a copy of *British Rate and Data* – commonly known as *BRAD*. This lists all UK trade magazines (plus newspapers, consumer magazines etc) and tells you *how often* they appear, *who* reads them, and *how much* it costs to advertise in them.
- Once you have found the trade magazine you want, write off for a free sample copy – you can ask for a subscription later.

NB: Most trade magazines are available on free subscription.

Louise runs a small firm that sells Christmas hampers and other gift items. To find new customers, she decides to target a specific industry where competition for business is fierce and where the value of her gifts (as a means of wooing customers) is likely to be most appreciated. She chooses the printing industry and starts drawing up a list of printing companies to sell to. In addition to consulting Kompass, she also gets hold of several trade magazines that cover the printing and packaging industries. By reading these, Louise not only gets to know who's who in the printing world, she also gets a 'feel' for how they operate and how they sell themselves to their customers. **Result?** She knows who to sell her hampers to, and how.

10. Get noticed!

How to canvass local home-owners

- Personal appearance counts! Carry a clipboard and either wear something formal and smart, or casual and bright. One very successful salesman whom I once knew used to wear a top-hat when canvassing!
- Carry some means of identity.
- Be patient! Allow an average of about four minutes per house (for average estates), more for upmarket houses.
- Be realistic! If you choose a reasonably convenient time to call, expect to speak to no more than about one in four homeowners.
- If the owner is out, leave your leaflet/sticker and arrange to call back at a more convenient time.
- Be prepared to sell if required! Carry a few testimonials with you, just in case.

A simple all-purpose canvassing method

- First, explain that you are not selling anything.
- Next, depending on what you sell, ask two basic questions:
  - — Who in the house normally buys your type of product/service?
  - — How likely are they to buy your sort of product, over (say) the next six months?
- Finally, give them one of your leaflets to look at, or (better still) a sticker to put up in their kitchen to remind them of who you are, what you do and how to contact you.

Result? You have a contact name and a rough idea of the level of their interest in your product – you can follow up this initial contact by phone at a later date. Meanwhile, they know who you are and what you have to offer: ie, you are noticed!

Rose owns a florist shop. Her get-noticed-campaign goes like this:

First, she orders 5000 leaflets targeted at householders. These list her products and explain that she will be calling shortly. **Next,** every Tuesday for four weeks, she delivers these leaflets to houses in selected streets, using the services of a group of students. **Finally,** every Wednesday, she loads up her small van with flowers, leaves her assistant to mind the shop and visits each householder in person. On each doorstep she asks three questions:

1. Do you want to buy any flowers?
2. Do you want to order any flowers for delivery over the next week or so?
3. Would you like me to call every month to show you what I've got?

Result? In her first four weeks she visits 600 householders, of whom 60 buy flowers immediately and a total of 150 ask her to call regularly. At this point, her sales barely cover her costs.

However, she repeats the exercise for 12 more weeks (in different suburbs) until she has 240 regular customers to call on. Now, she visits 60 of these customers every Wednesday and sells an average of £300 worth of flowers. Prior to festive occasions, this figure rises to £450. It has taken a lot of time and effort to get this far, but as Rose says – 'that's business!'

Be imaginative!

Door-to-door canvassing is only one method of getting noticed. There are many others. The trick is, be imaginative! Choose what is best for *you*.

Bugsy owns a small suburban firm that sells and repairs a range of electrical appliances. In order to get noticed by customers in his local neighborhood, he has his van resprayed a bright orange colour. Painted on each side of the car (in frog-green) is the following message: 'I fix anything electrical – TVs, Videos, Vacuum Cleaners, Washing Machines. For immediate service ring me (Bugsy) today on 234 5678.' **Result?** Within three months of this very visible vehicle being on the road, almost everyone in the area knows who Bugsy is and what he does.

Lofty installs satellite dishes, repairs roofs, gutters, gates and washing lines, sweeps chimneys, and gets rid of mice and spiders. To get noticed by his local customers, he decides to advertise his service where he knows they congregate and chat. First, he compiles a list of every hair salon within a five-mile radius. Second, he orders 200 A4 size bright yellow posters from his local printer. The poster is headlined: 'The next time you have a "nasty" job to do – call Lofty on 444 222.' Underneath, he lists all the nasty jobs he does. He then visits each hair salon on his list and asks the owner whether she will display his poster – 'as a service to their customers'. Most do. **Result?** Every day, Lofty's ad is noticed by dozens of new customers.

How to get noticed by other firms

There is only one really effective way to get noticed by a buyer who works for another firm: *go and see him!* Whatever the outcome of the meeting, by sitting down and discussing your product face to face with your buyer, you *will* be noticed. You are no longer simply a name or a voice at the end of the phone!

Face to face selling – the six golden rules

1. *Prepare thoroughly.*
   Re-read the first three chapters of this book: they tell you all you need to know about how to sell anything to anyone.

2. *Make human contact with your customer.*
   Don't behave like a robot! Adjust your approach to the human being in front of you. If you can establish a good personal rapport with him, you are halfway towards making a sale.

3. *Find out what his particular need is.*
   Don't say anything about your product until you have worked out what the customer's need is. To be on the safe side, summarise his need and repeat it back to him before starting your presentation.

4. *Explain how your product will satisfy his need.*
   Tailor your explanation to his need. Don't waffle. Show him hard evidence such as testimonials etc.

5. *Close the sale by helping him to say Yes.*
   Never ask whether he wants to buy; always assume he's going to buy – the only question is how much. And don't always wait for him to raise objections; if necessary, raise and answer them yourself.

6. *Avoid leaving loose ends.*
   — If the customer agrees to buy, take his order and arrange to phone back in the near future to see how things are going.
   — If he wants to consult his colleagues before buying,

then (a) ensure that you have covered all relevant matters; (b) give or fax him written details; and (c) arrange a specific time to phone back.

— If he decides not to buy, make sure you understand *why*. If you don't, you won't know how to change his mind in the future! Finally, before leaving, try to get him to agree to see you again in a few weeks time.

One business friend of mine (we'll call him Jonathan) has a particularly unusual method of getting noticed by his customers. Whenever he goes to an important meeting with a senior buyer, he takes a friend with him. During the meeting, this friend – who happens to be a brilliant caricaturist – does an impromptu caricature of the senior buyer sitting opposite. The finished drawing is then inscribed with the name of Jonathan's company and given to the buyer as a memento of the meeting. If necessary, Jonathan frames it and gives it to the buyer at the next meeting. **Result?** According to Jonathan, no buyer has ever forgotten him or his company!

A cheap alternative to visiting customers

If the customer is not worth a personal visit, send him a personal reminder of your firm instead.

Common items include T-shirts or mugs imprinted with your company name, logo and any other details. Typical cost: T-shirts printed front and back, from about £2 each for a minimum of 300; Mugs from about £1 each for a minimum of 500.

Conclusion – Don't blame the recession! Be positive!

Finding and selling to new customers is not always easy. However, in my experience, many businesspeople give up too quickly. *They seem to expect customers to find them!* When this doesn't happen, they shrug their shoulders and blame 'the recession'.

Don't make the same mistake! The world is full of new customers, but *you* have to find them!

8

Eight easy ways to get your customers to buy more

1. Give special attention to big-spending customers – or else!

Big-spending customers are dangerous: they can lure you into a false sense of security. Never take them for granted; instead, pamper them with good service. If you do, they'll spend even more; if you don't, then sooner or later they'll take their business elsewhere.

Sherlock is a self-employed private detective. He has 25 regular customers; mostly hire-purchase companies. Of these 25, all but one spend less than £500 per year with him, while one (a major bank) spends nearly £10,000. What's more, unlike the 24 smaller customers who need constant persuasion to give him work and constant reminders to pay their bills, his big customer gives him regular assignments and always pays on time. Alas, Sherlock starts to take this customer for granted. For example, instead of making regular personal visits to the boss to explain how things are going, he just speaks to the assistant on the phone. **Result?** One day he receives a letter from the bank terminating his contract. The bank's head office has given all its investigation work to a national detective agency.

Judy owns a dry-cleaning business. Most of her regular customers are private individuals. She has only five trade customers. However, these 5 account for 75 per cent of her total business, and one of them (a large Hotel) accounts for almost 30 per cent. Unlike Sherlock, Judy realises that her profit depends upon the goodwill of her big customers. Every week, therefore, she pays a short courtesy call on the manager of the hotel to check that her service is going smoothly and that he has no complaints. **Result?** When head office informs the hotel's manager that a cheaper contract has been negotiated with a national dry-cleaning firm, he opts to continue doing business with Judy.

Punch owns a small building firm. One of his most lucrative contracts is a building and decorating maintenance contract for a large warehousing company on the outskirts of town. Because it accounts for nearly 10 per cent of his turnover, Punch makes a big effort to ensure that all work is done promptly and to a high standard. He even hires a full-time carpenter to finish off a range of inessential jobs, to keep the customer more than satisfied. **Result?** When the customer decides to expand its offices, Punch gets the new building contract. What's more, he also asks for (and gets) a glowing testimonial from the customer, which he uses to win a large contract from another firm on the same industrial estate.

The moral? Big-spending customers need constant attention. Never take them for granted.

2. Pay attention to detail

If you have a small business you will usually have to be in four different places at once. As a result, you will often be tempted to cut corners. Be careful! Even tiny errors can sometimes cause disaster.

Lance owns a small painting and decorating business. One day he visits the maintenance manager of a large advertising agency, to quote for the job of redecorating 5000 square feet of offices. Because he is in a hurry, he has no time to change out of his overalls and paint-splattered shoes. **Result?** The maintenance manager is reluctant to show him around the offices (in case clients see him) and informs him that the painting contract has gone to another firm – all because Lance omitted to spend five minutes changing into something more respectable.

Tom owns a small computer software company. So does *Dick*. Both take stands at a business computer exhibition. During the show, they are visited by *Harry*, who wants them to write a software program for his telephone marketing company. He expects to pay about £2000. Because the show is very busy, he asks Tom and Dick to ring him the following week to make an appointment to visit him and give him separate quotes. Both take his details and agree to call. Unfortunately, while Tom makes a point of carefully writing Harry's details into a large file, Dick writes them on the nearest slip of paper. **Result?** Dick loses the slip containing Harry's details and with it, any chance of making a £2000 sale.

Zelda owns a hairdressing and beauty salon. Because her line of work is so competitive, she trains her receptionist to recognise customer's names and to make each caller feel special. **Result?** Customers prefer booking appointments with Zelda's salon.

The moral? Look after the little things – they can make a big difference! The newer your business, the more important this is. Be warned! According to experts, one of the quickest ways to lose business is not to return a customer's phone call.

3. Give customers *more* than they pay for!

This simple idea will always win you extra business. Customers never expect to get *more* than they pay for!

Simone owns a small French restaurant. At the end of each meal, she offers each customer an extra dessert – free of charge. **Result?** Customers show their appreciation by coming back and spending more.

Merlin owns a small firm that repairs and services cars. Each car he services is cleaned and valeted at no extra cost. **Result?** Customers keep coming back and spending more.

Joseph is a self-employed carpenter. Whenever he visits a customer's house to do a job, he brings his own vacuum cleaner with him. His aim is to leave things *tidier* than they were before he arrived! **Result?** Customers reward this extra effort by giving him all their carpentry work.

Marlene owns a small hotel. On arrival, she offers each single guest a free half-bottle of wine in the hotel bar and each couple a full bottle. **Result?** Her guests spend more time (and money) in the hotel bar/restaurant.

Dolly owns a ladies hairdressing shop. Because competition is fierce, she decides to offer customers something extra. So every Wednesday and Saturday she employs a student beautician to give all her customers a free 15-minute manicure. **Result?** Her new customers become regulars and her regulars stay loyal.

Delilah owns a different hairdressing business. To boost sales on Monday (her quietest day) she hires people to entertain her customers. At the moment she uses a palmist who spends about 15 minutes telling each customer their fortune. **Result?** The customers love it and most of them even leave an extra tip! At a net cost of about £20, Delilah converts a quiet day into a busy day and builds a loyal customer base into the bargain.

Stanley is a self-employed plumber. Like most tradesmen, he has two big problems. First, for every job he gets, he has to quote for about five others. Second, very few domestic customers stay loyal to one plumber, so repeat business is usually rare. In an attempt to solve these two problems, Stanley decides to offer something extra: he decides to *guarantee* every heating system he installs. He bluntly tells customers – if they have a problem, ring him straight away and he'll come and fix it for a nominal charge. To get the message across, he includes a written guarantee with every quote. **Result?** He gets more quotes accepted and more repeat business – his straight talk and his no-quibble guarantee gives him a clear edge over his competitors.

Zsa Zsa owns a ladies boutique. To keep her customers happy, she buys a large stock of a classic French perfume, rebottles it into smaller 10ml bottles and gives one away free with every purchase.

4. Offer additional services

By offering more you will sell more and give yourself an edge over your competitors.

Saul owns a laundrette, offering both do-it-yourself and service washes. Unfortunately, even though his washing machines are busy, sales are still too low for comfort. So one week, he spends most of his time discreetly watching his customers. He discovers that the laundrette is used by 40 (DIY) people every weekday and by 50 people a day on Saturdays and Sundays; ie, a total of 300 people per week. What else can he offer these 300 customers? He decides on two things: (1) a small range of newspapers and magazines; and (2) teas/coffees out of paper cups. **Result?** Within a month, he is selling a weekly average of 120 drinks (at 40p profit per drink) and 80 papers/magazines (at 30p profit) – a total of £72 extra profit per week! What's more, these extra services make his laundrette a more pleasant environment and so attract even more customers.

Flash Harry is a self-employed electrician. Because his is a very competitive trade, Flash is always looking to offer his customers something extra, both to make more money and to get repeat work. Every time he visits a house to repair an electrical item, he offers to sell and fit a burglar alarm or an intercom. Because he has been invited into the house and is seen to be trustworthy, (and because both products are quite appealing), his offer is often accepted. **Result?** He sells more and customers remember him.

Lofty (see p 88) is a self-employed handyman who installs TV aerials and satellite dishes. To impress customers and make a bit of extra money, he always asks them whether they have any other household 'nasties' that need doing. He gives them a leaflet explaining his extra services. These include checking roofs for faulty tiles; gutter-repair; rain-proofing wooden fences, gates etc; mending washing lines; getting rid of mice and spiders etc. Because he makes it so easy for customers to have these awkward jobs done, many of them say Yes to something – either then, or later. **Result?** His business increases.

Dot owns a small carpet-cleaning business. Because it takes her about five hours to finish a job, she can usually manage only one house per day. This often means that three hours are wasted, so Dot decides to offer something extra – both to help her customers and to boost her takings. She therefore asks each customer she visits whether they want their cars valeted, their windows cleaned or their attics/garages/garden sheds cleared out. Many customers are only too delighted to pay someone to have these jobs taken care of. At least a quarter of them say Yes to something extra. **Result?** Dot's sales go up.

Damon is a driving instructor. With every 12 lessons he offers an hour's free tuition on the highway code. **Result?** He gets more customers and a better success rate.

5. Take advantage of complaints

Don't see customer complaints as a problem: see them as an opportunity to sell more – if not straight away, then certainly in the future!

The 5 Finger Method of handling complaints

1. Ask the customer for his name, address and telephone number.
2. Thank him for drawing your attention to his problem, give him your name and tell him you will do your best to give him complete satisfaction.
3. Ask him for the details, then listen and don't interrupt. Let him get his story off his chest, no matter how garbled or nonsensical it sounds.
4. After he has finished, repeat the salient points back to him for confirmation and then deal with the complaint on its merits. If you need to check his story, say so and tell him that you will phone him back. If you/your firm is at fault try to give the customer immediate compensation.
5. Make a final gesture to regain the customer's goodwill; eg, if you/your firm are blameless write a letter expressing your personal regret at his misfortune – if necessary offer him a small extra discount or gift. If you are partly at fault, make a more generous gesture. Ideally, follow up your letter a few days later with a personal phone call.

Two reasons why you should pamper customers who complain

First, you can eliminate a lot of bad publicity. Experts say that customers who complain are likely to tell an average of 10 other people about their experience.

Second, you can gain loyal customers. Experts say that 66 per cent of all those who complain will buy from the same firm in the future, if their problem is resolved.

> *Tip: In my experience, the way you handle a customer's problem is a decisive factor in determining whether (and how much) he will buy from you in the future. If you respond positively, you will usually be able to sell him a lot more, no matter how bad your service has been; if you don't, you can usually kiss goodbye to any more business.*

I vividly remember one customer of mine, Jack, who owned a large computer shop in London. Jack ordered a brand new computer game from my distribution company for one of his customers, only to open it (in front of the customer) to find not a computer game inside but a mouldy cheese burger! Needless to say, he was not impressed. In fact he rang me up that instant with the full story. I didn't say anything for five minutes. (What *could* I say?) Finally, his insults and threats died down, whereupon I said something like:

> 'Jack, I'm not going to waste my breath telling you that we don't normally send out cheese burgers; instead, *let me tell you what I'm going to do to put things right.*'

I then suggested that he ring the customer to explain that he had spoken to the MD of the company responsible (ie, me), and that he had succeeded in getting the customer three free computer games (of his choice) by way of compensation.

As it happened, Jack's customer – who was in the shop when Jack rang me – happily agreed to my proposal. **Result?** Jack looked extra good in the eyes of his customer and (by way of thanks) became a regular buyer from my company from then on.

6. Get personal with your customers

We all prefer to buy things from people we feel comfortable with. In fact, according to experts, our personal relationship with the seller is a major factor in deciding which product to buy.

The moral? By improving your relationships with your own customers, you will increase your sales.

Kitty owns a city centre cafe. She believes that people prefer a cafe with a friendly atmosphere. She therefore makes a point of clearing many of the tables herself in a friendly, easy-going manner, and chats to her customers whenever she can. She also trains her staff to be as cheerful as possible, no matter how awful they may be feeling. **Result?** Even though Kitty offers the same service as many other cafes, her cafe is busier.

Mickey is an electrician. Whenever he does a domestic repair or installation he always takes the trouble to explain the job (eg, what the problem was) and to advise the customer how to keep an eye on things in the future. Unlike many of his fellows – who think that chatting to customers is a waste of valuable time – Mickey knows that a good relationship with a customer is worth a lot of future business. And he's right!

Minnie owns a small business which makes tailors' dummies for sale to large and small retailers. She often has to deal with senior buyers from larger firms. In order to develop a relationship with these buyers, she knows she has to treat them with *respect*. So, she always goes through the right channels and plans her calls carefully. Above all, she tries to present an image of calmness and reliability because she knows that senior buyers prefer to deal with someone who is capable of handling problems. **Result?** By showing her customers respect, she finds them easier to get to know and more receptive to her ideas.

Minnie treats her customers like human beings! For example:

* She always tries to meet them face to face.
* She asks about how they came to do their particular job.

- She asks about their families and/or their interests.
- She remembers and uses the information they give her, for example:
  — she sends them appropriate individual Christmas cards;
  — if she knows their birthday, she sends them a card;
  — she talks about things that she knows interest them;
  — she sends them occasional newspaper cuttings of things that she knows will amuse them.

Result? By being alert to the human element in business, Minnie has a good (and profitable) relationship with most of her customers.

7. Keep up-to-date with your market

Customers prefer to buy from someone who knows his trade, so if you want them to buy from *you* – keep up to date! Even if you are not interested in the latest technology or the latest products, you should know *something* about them.

- *Join your trade association.*
  Get the latest trade news and other benefits: (see page 83). Among other things, look out for alternative or cheaper suppliers.

- *Subscribe to your relevant trade magazines.*
  Most are free to trade personnel: (see page 86). In addition, most offer a free enquiry service, through which you may obtain news of new products and services coming on to the market. Keep a lookout for useful trade fairs and exhibitions.

- *Keep an eye on what your competitors are doing.*
  Contact them every few months to get a copy of their latest brochure etc, or get a friend to do it for you.

- *Maintain regular contact with your suppliers.*
  Suppliers are often an excellent source of information about new developments. Tap their brains.

- *Ideally, read the newspaper that is read by your customers.*
  Look out for news about the general likes and dislikes of your customers.

Heidi owns a city centre cafe. She has free subscriptions to a variety of catering magazines. One day she reads of a new microwave snack for vegetarians, called the 'Health Kebab' and immediately places an order. **Result?** The product's novelty value tempts more customers into her cafe and becomes the sort of small talking-point that gives her business an edge.

Conrad makes a variety of leather belts which he sells to a range of different shops. Every autumn, he makes a point of reading all the women's fashion magazines to find out what people will be wearing the following year. For instance, last autumn he discovered that thin, coloured belts were going to be all the rage: he therefore altered his manufacturing accordingly. **Result?** Shops take him more seriously than other suppliers. If he says a particular belt will sell – they believe him.

Ethel owns a clothes shop for toddlers. Every month she reads a number of magazines for wholesalers. One day, she reads about a forthcoming auction of bankrupt stock which includes several thousand pairs of mittens for toddlers. She goes along and buys them for a knockdown price. **Result?** She sells them (for a small profit) at a ridiculously low price – using them as a loss leader to attract extra customers into her store.

8. Never stop selling yourself to a customer!

A sale to a customer should be the *beginning* of your business relationship with that person, not the end of it.
    Here are four things that you should do:

1. *After each sale: get the customer's details and update them.*
   Keep a card on each customer. Update it with details of each sale, or contact or new address.

2. *After each sale: ask for a testimonial.*
   Don't be shy about asking each satisfied customer for a note testifying to the quality of your product or service. If you suspect that the customer can't be bothered to write one himself, type one out for him and get him to sign it. If possible, also ask for referrals.

3. *After each sale: stay in touch with your customers.*
   Make a courtesy phone call to them at least once every 4–8 weeks.
   — Ask what you can do for them. *Re-sell yourself!*
   — Update them on any improvements in your service.

4. *Follow up your courtesy phone calls with a letter.*
   Remember the power of the written word!
   — Include one or two paragraphs promoting your service and reminding them *why they should buy from you!* Never assume that, because they have bought from you once (or more) they will automatically buy again.
   — Make it clear that you welcome any suggestions for how you can improve your service.

D'Arcy owns a small new estate agents. His services include locating as well as selling and surveying property. By teaming up with a small firm of jewellers he also values jewellery and other precious items. His after-sales selling goes like this. Whenever he sells a house:

- He records the new addresses of both vendor and purchaser.
- He asks each of them for a testimonial. These are then framed and hung on the walls of his office.
- He also asks the vendor whether he knows anyone else who is thinking of putting a house on the market.
- Eight weeks after the sale, he telephones both vendor and purchaser to ask how they are getting on. In addition, he

explains that he also locates property and values jewellery, in case they ever need either of these services.

- One week later, he sends them a two-page letter giving full details of all his services.
- Three months later, he phones again to see how they are and whether they know anyone who is thinking of selling a house.
- He repeats this exercise every six months.

Result? By staying in touch with all his customers in this way, he greatly increases his chance of doing future business with them and their friends. *Plus,* he also gets to hear of any houses for sale *before* they appear on the market.

Barry is a plumber. Whenever he visits a private customer to do a job, he always asks what plumbed appliances are in the house (washing machines, spin dryer, boiler, central heating system etc). He tries to find out from the customer when each appliance was last serviced and makes a note in his file. Finally, he also records the customer's name, address, telephone number. (After doing this for two years, he not only has a long list of customers, he also has a list of their appliances and a note of when each needs servicing.) Then every weekend, he combs through these lists to find which customer needs an appliance checking. He telephones/writes to each one with a reminder. **Result?** He gets a constant stream of repeat business.

Benazir owns a small firm that distributes high quality imported ladies underwear to a range of large and small retailers. Although she is now relatively established, she has four well-established regular customers who still buy from her at a large discount – the same discount she offered them when she started her business. Now, she wants to reduce that discount and get them to buy at normal prices. This is what she does.

- Every month for four months, she sends all her customers a personal letter (headed – 'Our Commitment To Our Customers') informing them of small improvements in her service and updating them on her new products. She follows up each letter with a phone call to ask how the customer is doing and whether they are happy with her service.

- Then, she arranges a personal appointment with each of the four big-discount customers, at which she puts her case as follows. **First,** she thanks them for their continuing business. **Second,** she explains that her aim is to constantly improve her overall service and gives examples of what she has achieved to date. **Third,** she says that to maintain this level of customer service, she must phase out her larger discounts and ask them to pay more. **Fourth,** she reassures each of them that they will continue to receive special attention due to their longstanding relationship with her.

Result? The first two customers agree to her new prices without any problem. The third says he may be forced to order less in future (although as it turns out, he doesn't). The fourth cancels all his future orders and buys elsewhere, but as Benazir knows, a customer who buys on price alone is not worth losing sleep over and the reduced discounts will minimise the loss of sales.

Cuthbert owns a small interior-design business. He sells his skills to private homeowners as well as to trade customers such as shops, restaurants, hotels etc. As soon as he finishes a job to the customer's satisfaction, he asks the customer to draft a testimonial letter of recommendation which he (Cuthbert) may show to third parties. **Result?** Cuthbert has a massive file of testimonials which he uses to impress both his bank manager (when he needs a loan) and his new customers!

Zena is a music tutor. Whenever any of her pupils pass a music exam, she asks their parents whether they would be kind enough to write a short testimonial for her (most are only too happy to oblige). Zena then frames a photocopy of each testimonial and hangs it on the walls of her music room. **Result?** Whenever potential new pupils visit her to discuss her tutor service, they see a roomful of testimonials praising Zena's tutorship. And if Zena visits them instead, she carries the originals in a file.

Fritz is a self-employed dog-trainer. Whenever he trains a dog, he asks its owner whether he knows anyone else whose dog might benefit from being trained. (Most owners usually give him at least one or two names.) He then contacts each of them, using the referee's name as an introduction. **Result?** On average, from every three satisfied customers, Fritz obtains another booking.

Yvonne owns a ladies hairdressing salon. Every time she (a) restyles a customer's hair; or (b) gives a customer a new colour or wave, she phones them at home a few days later, to check they are happy with their new look. Usually they are, but even if they are not, they very much appreciate being asked. **Result?** They stay loyal to Yvonne – after all, how many other hairdressers would bother with such thoughtful after-sales service?

Checklist

If nothing else, follow these two rules:

1. *Stay in touch with your customers.*
    Why? Because they are your best source of extra sales.
2. *Never take your present customers for granted.*
    Keep impressing them. Keep spoiling them. Above all, *keep selling to them!*

9

How to sell like a professional over the telephone

The No 1 secret: prepare, prepare, prepare!

Never dial a customer before you have a rough idea of what you will say. Only amateurs dial first and then think about what to say – *professionals know what they are going to say before they dial.*

Four simple things you should prepare before dialling:

1. *Questions you wish to put to the customer.*
    If you need information from your customer, jot down a few questions in advance.

2. *An outline of what you want to say.*
    Make a list of the points you want to cover and the order in which you want to raise them. If you need to be able to quote specific details, have them in front of you.

3. *The answers to any obvious questions that may be raised.*
    Don't rely on your natural ability to handle tricky questions; prepare a few answers in advance. (See pages 16–17 for a list of typical customer concerns.)

4. *The close.*
    Decide what you want to achieve (ie, a sale), then plan a fall-back objective in case your main one fails (eg, a call-back or appointment).

The two biggest mistakes that amateurs make over the phone

Amateurs talk too fast

Most amateurs gabble on the phone. As a result, their listeners switch off. Don't gabble! For instance, always talk more slowly to an unfamiliar buyer than you would to a friend. Remember, it takes a lot more concentration to listen to a strange voice. *So if your customer has never heard your voice before, speak slowly to allow him to absorb what you are saying.*

> *Fact: when anyone picks up the phone and hears on unfamiliar voice, they usually need about 10–15 seconds to 'wake up' – ie, orientate themselves. So, when calling a customer for the first time, avoid giving him any information during these first few seconds – he will only ask you to repeat yourself.*

Compare these two different approaches to beginning a conversation with a strange buyer

The amateur:

Mr Buyer:	Hello, Mr Buyer speaking.
Amateur:	Hello Mr Buyer. Joe Smith of Fabulous Foods here . . .
Mr Buyer:	(Unable to adjust to what he has just been told) Er . . . I'm sorry, who's calling?

The professional:

Mr Buyer:	Hello, Mr Buyer speaking.
Professional:	(Deliberately wasting time to allow the buyer to wake up) Hello, is that Mr Buyer?
Mr Buyer:	Yes it is.
Professional:	(Deliberately waffling) Hello, Mr Buyer, (pause) I don't think that I've spoken to you

> before, (pause) my name is Joe Smith (pause),
> I'm the Managing Director of Fabulous
> Foods . . .

While the amateur rattles off his name and company name within about 8 seconds of Mr Buyer picking up the phone, the professional takes nearly twice as long.

The moral: Give your listener time to wake up: if you do you will create a better first impression.

Amateurs lose the attention of their buyer

To avoid this, always adjust what you say (and how you say it) to the *individual*, and be imaginative!

Two simple ways to keep the attention of your buyer:

1. *Be relevant.*
    Don't waste time explaining how your product can help every Tom, Dick and Harriet. Get to the point: tell the customer how *he* will benefit. And be specific.
      For example, imagine you own a motorbike courier service. You telephone a customer (the MD of a local secretarial employment agency) to interest her in using your courier service. Don't just tell her that you charge less than your rivals: *explain exactly how this will benefit her!* For example, tell her that if she uses your service three times a week, she is likely to save herself about £500 a year on her normal courier bills – enough to buy herself ten extra £50 classified ads!

2. *Create visual images.*
    Describe real-life situations that explain the benefits of your product or service.
      For example, imagine you sell fax machines to small firms, from your office equipment shop. Bert, a small wine merchant, rings you for details.

- Don't just tell Bert how good your fax machines are, or how good your after-sales service is: illustrate your point with a *real-life example!* For example, paint a picture of Bert trying to telephone a new French wine supplier. He rings on Monday but the supplier is out; he rings on Tuesday but the supplier is busy; on Wednesday, he gets through but the supplier can't speak English! Result, Bert has *wasted time and money for nothing.* With a fax, he could probably have sent a message in French on the Monday and had a reply by Tuesday morning.

- As for why he should buy his fax from you; give him another concrete example: describe a situation where he needs to send a series of important faxes but can't because his fax machine has gone wrong – as all fax machines occasionally do.

   Explain that if he buys his machine from you, he can just dial your special *hotline repair number* and get same day service or replacement. However, if he buys his machine from another office equipment supplier, he might find their phones constantly engaged, or that another firm does their repairs and is too busy to help, or that they are closed on Saturday, and so on.

For example, imagine you own a small building firm. You telephone a private customer to discuss your quote to build a new front porch. The customer says that your (reasonable) quote is too expensive.

- Don't give the customer chapter and verse about which materials cost what price. This is not likely to mean much to him.

- Instead, give him a *real-life situation* to think about. For example, tell him he can probably get a cheaper quote, but ask him how he is likely to feel if his cheaper porch starts to let in draughts or develop condensation. Tell him that 'your' porch will still be perfectly OK in five years' time, whereas a cheaper one might need more money spent on it *next year*.

Tell him that cheaper builders don't stay in business very long, so when he rings up his cheaper builder to complain – the builder will probably have disappeared.

How to sell to companies over the phone: the '3 Call Approach'

Most company buyers do not buy things from strangers in the space of a single phone call – especially strangers who run small firms. You will therefore need to make at least three calls, possibly more.

Call No 1 – find out who to speak to

How not to do it

Salesperson:	'Hello, can I speak to whoever is in charge of buying your computer stationery, please?'
Receptionist:	'Just a moment...' (She checks with someone.) 'I'm sorry, I'm told we don't need any at the moment. Goodbye.'

A better approach

To avoid this happening to you, instead of asking to speak to the buyer, say simply that you want to send him some information.
Say something like:

'Hello, I wonder if you could help me please. I'd like to send some information to the person who usually buys your computer stationery. Could you give me his name please?'

Result? Nine times out of ten you will be given the buyer's name (eg, Mr Hedgehog).

Call No 2 – get past the secretary and speak to the buyer

When you ring back, say to the receptionist:

'Hello, Mr Hedgehog please.'

You do not ask whether Mr Hedgehog is in, or whether it is possible to speak to him; you simply give his name. **Result?** Nine times out of ten you will be put through to Mr Hedgehog's secretary.

When you get through to the secretary, it is absolutely essential to avoid giving her the impression that you are *unprofessional or likely to waste her boss's time.* Therefore:

• Be friendly and polite.
• Explain clearly why you want to speak to the buyer.
• Emphasise that you will be very brief.

Result? As a rough guide:

• About 3 times out of 10, you are put through.
• About 4 times out of 10, you are asked to call back and you are then put through on your return call. (My advice: ask for a specific time to call back.)
• About 3 times out of 10, you will find it difficult to get through – the secretary always claims the buyer is busy. (My advice: either, ring the buyer at a quite time, eg, 8.15 am or 6.00 pm, or write a letter to the buyer, then follow this up with a call.)

What to say to the buyer

When you get through to your buyer, try the following approach.

1. *Introduce yourself.*
   Give your name, your company name and say what it is you

sell. Emphasise that you will only take up two or three minutes of his time.

2. *Reassure him.*
   Explain that the purpose of your call is to introduce yourself and to arrange to send him some information – not to go into detail about your product.

3. *Question him.*
   Say that – if it's OK with him – you would like to ask him a few questions about his firm, for example . . . (at this point, ask a few prepared questions to try and discover to what extent he needs your product – for suggestions, see page 18).

4. *Arrange to send written details.*
   Say that you would like to send him written information.

5. *Arrange a call-back/appointment.*
   Briefly arrange a specific time to ring him back and/or to see him in person. If sending details, leave him a maximum of 48 hours to study them.

Call No 3 – make your sales presentation and get the order

What to say to the buyer

- *Reintroduce yourself.*
  Briefly remind the buyer of your previous conversation. Mention sending him details, but don't ask if he has studied them: assume he has.

- *Confirm his requirements.*
  Briefly go over what he told you about his requirements for your product. For example, if selling ceramic tiles to a DIY chain-store, say something like:

'From what you told me, Mr Hedgehog, I gather that you're looking for high quality tiles with designs that are likely to appeal to as wide an audience as possible. Is that about right?' (NB: If it isn't, he will tell you!)

- *Show how your product meets those particular requirements.*
  As recommended (page 29), use the 1:2:3 Method — (1) Make your point; (2) Back it up with evidence; (3) Show how this helps the customer.

- *Close the sale.*
  If you can close the sale there and then, fine; if not, find out *why* the buyer is still unconvinced. Once you know the reason, you can devise an answer to it.

- *Try to get something from every customer!*
  For example, if you can't close the sale and get an order:
  — Arrange a specific time to call back;
  — Arrange an appointment to discuss things further; or
  — Arrange to call back in a month's time.

  NB: *Re-read Chapters 1 to 3 in connection with this section.*

How to cold-call private individuals – the 4 key steps

The following method is designed to help you sell to *private individuals to whom you have never spoken before.* Use it as a general guideline and adapt it to your particular situation.

1. *Find a list of names and phone numbers (see page 71).*
   Unless you are selling a particularly expensive product or service, you need an *absolute minimum* of 500 names. Ideally, you should have between 1000 and 1500.
   The more selective the list, the better. For example, if you sell furniture, make sure your list has a high proportion of house-owners; if you sell a luxury item, make sure your list contains high-earners, and so on.

2. *Decide on a product to sell.*
   Ideally, sell (or lead with) a *standardised* product: eg, if you sell paint-brushes, standardise them by making up a mixed pack of 10, containing 3 big, 4 medium and 3 small ones and

so on. If you really want to sell different coloured paint, *lead* with your pack of brushes, *then* talk about paint.

3.   *Design a sales script.*
      A script is essential – you cannot sell successfully to large numbers of telephone customers without one.
      Although most scripts share many of the same basic features, their exact content will depend upon what *objective* you wish to achieve; eg, a one-call sale, a two-call sale, or an appointment.

Bob owns a small DIY shop. He has just bought a large load of discounted paint brushes direct from the manufacturer, which he divides into mixed packs of 10 and 20 brushes. He designs a one-call sales script to help him sell these packs to local homeowners. It goes like this:

First: He introduces himself.

'Hello, is that Mr/Mrs Smith? This is Bob from DIY Delight – the bright yellow shop next to the main library – you know the shop don't you?'

If the customer says no, Bob says:

'It's probably the best-value DIY shop in the area.'

Note: Bob immediately presents himself as a visible local trader.

Second: He asks a question to exclude redundant customers.

'Do you ever do any occasional painting or do you ever need to touch up any peeling paintwork in your house?'

If the customer says no, Bob says:

'Well if you do, please drop into the shop won't you. Goodbye.'

Note: Bob is not interested in persuading customers to buy something that they have no use for.

Third: He outlines his product and checks for interest.

'Great, because I have a very special paintbrush offer at the moment – I'm selling £35 worth of top quality paintbrushes at only £13.99 – would you like to hear the details?'

Note: He does not ask: 'Do you want to buy some brushes?' or even 'Are you interested?' It is too soon to ask for such a definite commitment.

If the customer says no, Bob says:

'Before I go, is there any DIY equipment (gives 2–3 suggestions) that you *would* be interested in hearing more about?'

If the customer still says no, Bob says:

'Well if you change your mind, pop into the shop: you'll be very welcome. Goodbye.'

Fourth: He briefly describes his product, ending on a question.

'OK, the brushes are very tough, they're British-made and they come in a complete range of sizes, right down to the very small gloss-ones – you know the ones I mean, don't you?'

Note: The question is rhetorical – it does not matter whether the customer knows about small brushes or not. The only reason Bob asks it is to keep his listener involved.

Fifth: He makes a specific offer and tries to close the sale.

'OK, I'm selling them in two different packs, each containing a mixture of sizes: the first contains 10 brushes (pause) and sells for £13.99; the second contains 20 brushes (pause) and sells for £22.99. Which one would you like – the 10 pack or the 20 pack?'

If the customer says neither, Bob says:

'Well if you change your mind or you need any other DIY stuff, pop into the shop: you'll be very welcome. Goodbye.'

If the customer says 'How do I pay?' or 'What about money?' Bob says:

'Don't worry about that, we'll deal with that in a moment.'

Note: Bob always discusses the details of payment or delivery etc after the customer has decided to buy.

Sixth: He wraps up the details.

Once the customer has chosen his preferred pack of brushes, Bob says:

'Right. You can pay for them in three different ways – whichever is most convenient for you. You can either pay by credit card, or by cheque or by cash – which do you prefer?'

If credit card:	Bob takes the details and arranges delivery of the brushes by first class post.
If cheque/cash:	Bob arranges to visit the customer's house the same evening to deliver the brushes and pick up payment.

Tip: Whatever script you use, keep modifying it until you are happy with it.

4. *Organise yourself – aim for 40 phone calls per hour*
    Don't bother trying this sales method unless you can make *at least 40 calls per hour*. Why not? Because only by making this number of calls will you develop the required rhythm

or momentum. Ideally, you should make 50+ calls per hour, but 40 is sufficient to start with.

In order to make 40 calls per hour you must be organised! Have your list of names and numbers ready in front of you; have pen and paper handy to record your sales, and *keep dialling!*

Bob, our man with the brushes, organises himself as follows:

• He only starts calling when his list contains at least 1000 contacts. He usually calls about 50 numbers per hour for three hours a day, two days a week. A list of 1000 names therefore takes him a month to get through.
• As he works his way through the list, he does two things: (a) he records any sales he makes; and (b) he crosses out those numbers on his list that are disconnected.
• When he comes to the end of his list, he calls everyone *once more* (except for those who have already bought) and then bins it.
• He doesn't waste time waiting for people to answer the phone! After five rings he disconnects.
• He never sends out any literature. Either customers are interested in what he has to say, or they are not.

Result? Bob averages about 5–7 sales (or approx £100) per hour. Although his success rate is good, his profits could be higher. To boost his profits in the future, Bob intends to make three improvements:

• He plans to source more profitable products.
• He plans to recruit and train two youngsters to sell over the phone.
• He plans to draw up a catalogue of all his shop products, which he can then mailshot to his growing list of customers and follow up by phone.

How professionals use the phone

Earle is a self-employed chimney sweep. He spends every Monday on the phone, selling his service to local householders. He gets their numbers from various sources, including phone books, the library and the local community register. His script is very short and begins: 'Hello. I wonder if I can help you. My name is Earle – I'm a qualified chimney sweep. Do you ever need your chimneys swept?' **Result?** He creates his own new business.

Nye is a self-employed plasterer. Every three weeks, he spends an entire day on the phone talking to large and medium-sized builders about sub-contracting opportunities. **Result?** By keeping in regular contact with these companies, his name is always on their list of people available to hire.

Maximillian owns a small bookshop. Twice a week, between 9 and 10 am, he telephones local firms to ask them whether they need any business books (on sales, export regulations etc) or HMSO statistical publications, to help them in their business. **Result?** Maximillian's book sales rise.

Axel is a butcher. He spends every Monday morning on the phone, talking to local hotels and restaurants about his meat delivery service. **Result?** His regular telephone work ensures a steady trickle of new customers.

'Snapper' Sid owns a city centre camera shop. In the back room, he employs four commission-only salespeople who telephone local householders to offer a range of different services, including cut-price family portraits, wedding photos and colour film. **Result?** His sales organisation produces a steady flow of cash and keeps his camera shop ahead of his rivals.

Lonnie owns a small printing company. In order to generate new business, he trains one of his young printing technicians to telephone local firms to arrange appointments for him (Lonnie) to sell his printing services. **Result?** Lonnie is free to devote all his time to selling.

Holly owns a small city centre florist/plant shop. To increase her sales, she regularly contacts local firms to introduce them to her service. Usually she talks to the managing director's secretary and suggests that whenever the firm needs to buy Christmas gifts for local customers, or entertain female customers, or give out staff prizes and so on, it should contact her first. **Result?** By using the phone to promote her business, Holly sells more.

The phone is a powerful sales instrument: use it!

- Don't wait for customers to come to you – give them a ring!
- If you don't know how to use the phone – learn how!
- If you can't use the phone – employ someone who can!

The moral? Don't ignore the power of the phone!

For a comprehensive guide to selling over the phone, read *Secrets of Telephone Selling*, also by Neil Johnson and published by Kogan Page.

10

Look after your No 1 sales asset – your time!

If you run a business, your most valuable sales asset is your time. Make the most of it and you will sell more; squander it and you will lose money.

How to save 49 complete working days a year

Save 6 days a year by planning your week

The easiest way to waste time is *not* to plan your week. If this sounds like you, here are a couple of suggestions:

- Buy a desk diary. Set aside one quiet hour per week to make a weekly plan.
- Jot down in your diary exactly what you want to do and when. Include names and phone numbers of who to call.
- Check the previous week's diary for things that remain undone.

Remember: running a business often requires you to coordinate the actions of other (less-organised) people. You can do this much more efficiently if you plan in advance (a) exactly what needs to be done; and (b) the order in which it needs to be done.

Result? By making a written plan, not only will you stop 'forgetting' things, you will also save yourself at least one hour's wasted time per week; ie, more than six complete working days per year!

Save 10 days a year by always having a notebook and pen handy

Probably more sales time is lost 'looking for a name or telephone number' than for any other reason.

The moral? When you need to remember something during the day: write it down in your notebook.

This alone will probably save you 20 minutes per day – that's 10 complete working days per year!

Save 13 days a year by controlling your incoming phone calls

Don't waste time answering unnecessary phone calls. Simply tell anyone who is due to ring you to phone back between, for example, 9 am and 10 am. Then if anyone (except of course, a customer) rings you after 10 am, explain you are busy and ask them to call back the next day between 9 and 10. **Result?** Instead of being controlled by incoming calls, *you* control *them*. In my experience, this action will save you at least 25 minutes per day – that's 13 complete working days per year!

Save 7½ days a year by calling important people before they call you

If you run a business, you are bound to have a number of 'important' customers or suppliers who must be kept happy at all times. In practice, this often requires you to hang around waiting for them to call. Here's how to handle them:

- Make a list of the names and phone numbers of these people.
- Make a note to ring each person at regular, set intervals.

Result? You demonstrate a high level of service *and* you do it at your own convenience; ie, you minimise time wasted hanging around waiting for an 'important' call to come through. I estimate that this will save you an average of at least 15 minutes per day; ie, 7½ complete working days per year.

Save 5 days a year by paying attention to your paperwork

You have sales/purchases to record and petty cash to account for. In addition, you may have wages to pay, VAT payments to record and various other bits of paper floating about. Keep it under control – if you don't, you will waste a huge amount of time.

For example:

* Set aside 15 minutes a day, to sort it out;
* Advertise for a part-time book keeper; or
* Give the job to a local accountant.

15 minutes per day is a small price to pay for accurate, up to date records. What's more, by doing something like this, I estimate you will save yourself at least five complete working days which you will probably have to spend getting things under control, at a later date.

Save 8 days a year by buying a fax machine

Once you have a fax machine, you can save at least 15 minutes a day writing purchase orders (during office hours) or running to catch the last post – to name but two improvements. Besides, if you deal regularly with other companies, you can't do business without a fax machine. Contact a local dealer for details.

If at all possible, computerise your business!

Unless your turnover is extremely small, you must think seriously about computerising your business, for a number of reasons.

Computers can save you (literally) months of time

- Letters, mailshots, budgets and forecasts, quotations can be written, corrected, altered, printed and reprinted much faster.
- Information can be retrieved instantly.
- All financial accounts and/or all product stores can be updated faster and more efficiently.

Computers can help you perform otherwise impossible tasks

For example:

- You (and your competitors) may think that a sale worth £20 is not worth a written quotation which may take you 1½ hours to prepare. However, by simply amending a standard quote stored on your computer, you might complete the job in a mere 10 minutes. **Result?** You quote for the sale: your competitors don't.
- You (and your competitors) may only produce a product list once every three months. Producing a new one at more regular intervals may be impractical, due to the time needed to prepare it. However, by storing your product list on your computer, you might be able to produce a new version every month. **Result?** You keep your customers up to date: your competitors don't.

Computers make your business look more professional

You will not impress a bank manager with an untidy or inaccurate sales forecast. Neither will you impress a customer with a letter blotched with correction fluid. Indeed, one such bad impression may cost you the price of a brand new computer system!

Similarly, you will not impress a customer who asks for an instant balance of his account by keeping him waiting while you perform a series of calculations at the other end of the phone.

The fact is, many customers expect a professional firm to be computerised and some won't even deal with you unless you are.

What will a computer do for your business?

What a computer will do for you depends upon what software you put into it. For example:

- A *wordprocessing* software program helps you to automate all your general typing work – eg, letters, quotes, mailshots etc.
- A *spreadsheet* program helps you to automate all your general forecasting – eg, future sales/cashflow budgeting.
- A *database* program helps you to automate customer files and instantly recall whatever you store.
- An *accounts* program automates your sales/purchase/cash ledgers as well as invoices, credit notes, statements, wages, VAT etc.

How to decide what sort of computer equipment to buy

- *Step 1*
  Visit your local bookshop; buy a simple guide to computers.

- *Step 2*

  Ask a friend or acquaintance for advice on what to buy. Ideally choose another business person.

- *Step 3*

  Visit your local business-computer dealer and ask him. Having a good local dealer is very important, not only because he is well placed to install and support your machine, but also because (ideally) you should buy everything from one source. (When visiting your dealer, be prepared to answer two key questions: (a) *What office tasks* do you want your computer to perform? (b) *How much* do you want to spend?)

An all-in computer system for your small business for about £1400

Subject to the advice of your local dealer, here are my recommendations for what to buy.

Computer

- **Key factor:** it must be powerful enough to do a range of tasks, including some which you may not yet have thought of!
- **My advice:** choose a 486 machine (ie, with a 486 processor) which has a *minimum* of 4 Megabytes of RAM and a *minimum* of 200 Megabytes of Hard Disc. Typical brand names include Compaq, Dell, Gateway 2000 and IBM. Cost: although you can pay much more, aim to spend about £900. (Note: be sure to ask your supplier for an *on-site warranty*.)

Printer

- **Key factors:** (a) it must make your printed material *look good;* (b) it must be *fast enough* for your needs. For these reasons, beware cheap printers.

- **My advice:** choose an *InkJet* printer (sometimes called BubbleJet). Typical models include Hewlett Packard HP 520 and the Canon BJ 200. Cost: about £200.

Software

Basically, software is what you see on the screen.

- **Key factors:** (a) it must be easy to understand and simple to use; (b) it must be capable of doing the things you want; (c) ideally, it should be installed into your computer, by the supplier, prior to purchase.
- **My advice:** Of all the excellent software available (which no doubt your dealer will explain) my personal advice is as follows:
  — For all your initial software needs (except accounts) choose *Microsoft Works 3.0* (not 2.0 or less). This enables you to perform a wide range of wordprocessing, spreadsheet and database activities. Cost: about £100. However, in practice, many suppliers give it away free when you buy certain computers.

  The moral? Shop around!

  — For your initial accounts needs, choose *Instant Accounting* by Sage. Cost: usually about £100+.

Note: when you buy, ask your dealer to install your software on the computer's Hard Disc.

- **An important extra**
  Buy a *Tape Streamer* (or Tape Drive) and ask to have it fitted. This is a back-up device, to avoid losing the information stored in your computer if electrical disaster strikes. It's worth remembering that, within a few months, the information on your computer will be worth a lot more than the computer itself! Cost: about £150 (including fitting). You will also need at least three tapes at about £20 each.

Running costs

These include annual insurance and/or warranty, plus computer stationery and ink. Ask your dealer for an estimate.

After you buy your software, learn how to use it!

Don't just rely on its accompanying manual – go out and buy a book on it. Then spend some time familiarising yourself with it.

Computerising your business – a final word

Computerising a business takes time and effort. As well as getting used to the software, you will also have to type all your business data (including customer information, product details etc) into the computer's memory, in order to get it to work for you! Nevertheless, if you choose your computer sensibly, learn how to use its software and don't expect too many miracles, you will wonder how you ever managed without one!

Conclusion – a small business is only as good as its owner!

Your business is driven by *you* – nobody else. The more time you can save, by organising and planning your week, the more time you can devote to selling your way to success. I wish you luck!

Further reading from Kogan Page

Auer, J T: *Inspired Selling: A Book of Ideas, Opportunities and Renewal*

Denny, Richard: *Selling to Win: Tested Techniques for Closing the Sale*

Golis, Christopher C: *Empathy Selling: The Powerful New Technique for the 1990s*

Hopkins, Leon: *Budgeting for Business Cash Flow And How To Improve It*

Johnson, Neil: *How to Sell More The Secrets of Telephone Selling*

Ley D Forbes: *The Best Seller*

Sadgrove, Kit: *Seductive Selling*

Vicar, Robert: *First Division Selling Prospecting for Customers*

A full list of books for the small firm is available from the publisher.